SHOP DESIGN

Edition 2013

Author: Carles Broto

Editorial coordination: Jacobo Krauel

Graphic design & production: Pablo Polcán

Collaborators: Oriol Vallés, graphic designer & Roberto Bottura, architect

Text: Contributed by the architects, edited by William George

© **Linksbooks**

Jonqueres, 10, 1-5

08003 Barcelona, Spain

Tel.: +34-93-301-21-99

info@linksbooks.net

www.linksbooks.net

When designing commercial spaces it is necessary to consider not just the types of activities that will be carried out in them, but also the different locations, functions and environments that they will require. All commercial premises, however, need a basic infrastructure that creates an efficient working environment and facilities that ensure excellent customer service. There have been considerable developments in the area of commercial spaces in recent years, mainly caused by the trend towards increasing numbers of shopping centers appearing in cities, following the influence of the American model.

The proliferation of these centers has gone hand in hand with developments in new ways of understanding commercial premises. These include changes in the way internal spatial divisions are conceived (they were far more schematic and conventional in the past), the systematic use of light and color as integral elements of the architecture, the use of prefabricated materials and the widespread tendency to use transparent spaces, with few visible separations.In order to provide a representative vision of the most innovative recent designs, we have tried as far as possible to show the great diversity of commercial spaces and their almost infinite decorative possibilities, as a kind of graphic guide to current and future trends in interior design for customer service spaces. We have also made a considerable effort to show not just the overall design of each project, but also the most significant construction details, which in some cases are an essential part of the character of the finished space. For this reason we have included all kinds of graphic material, such as photographs, plans, elevations and axonometric views and sketches, together with a description of the work as it was conceived by the architect.

LEONG LEONG

3.1 Phillip Lim

Cheongdam-Dong, Seoul, South Korea

Photographs: Iwan Baan, Leong Leong

This project, located in Seoul's premiere fashion district Cheongdam-Dong, is a single store within 3.1 Phillip Lim's global roll-out campaign, which will include many international locations. Aware of the inevitable repetition that is necessary for such a commercial expansion, the designers thought of the typology of a flagship store as being characterized by the simultaneous need for sameness and difference. Typically, the consistent repetition of brand traits is necessary to reinforce an identity, while novelty can refresh the aura and desire for the brand. In this particular case the client, a relatively new fashion house, emphasized the need to establish a legible consistency in order to unify the different existing stores in New York, Los Angeles, and Tokyo.

The designers opted for organizational maneuvers that could respond to specific constraints encountered in different store locations and contexts. The Los Angeles flagship was used as a kind of base diagram to which a combination of additional features could be applied in order to exploit the constraints in the Seoul site.

For example, the smaller footprint of the existing structure in Seoul is accommodated by literally cropping the continuous curving wall of the Los Angeles store into a smaller frame, creating four enclaves. The enclaves were stacked to fit within the two levels of retail space. Each enclave accommodates a different use: display, fitting rooms, storage, and stairs to the upper floor retail space. Since the existing space also had extremely low ceiling heights the designers extended two of the enclaves vertically to cut out double height spaces, one of which became the new staircase to the upper floor. The main entrance to the store is also a type of enclave, cropped and recessed from the façade with a continuous glass storefront.

The existing perimeter walls are lined in mirror, multiplying the cropped curving wall into a field of enclaves extending infinitely in the reflection of the mirror. While the Los Angeles store uses mirror to double the enclosed spaces between the curving wall and the existing wall, the Seoul store uses mirror to expand a continuous visual field of space in which the cropped enclaves float.

The 20 m (65 ft) high façade wraps the existing building with a supple gradient of convex concrete panels. The eight different panel types progressively flatten as they climb the façade, the supple texture of the façade fading into the city's often overcast, gray sky.

Architecture:
LEONG LEONG

Lead designers:
Dominic Leong, Chris Leong

Project team:
Christa Mohn, Scott Rominger,
Cody Zalk, Debbie Chen

Structural engineer:
Barun Structure Engineering

General contractor:
Sung Ho-Yoon / Dadam S.D.

Wallpaper:
Wook Kim

Client:
3.1 Phillip Lim

Floor area:
543 sqm (5,850 sqft)

The designers opted for organizational maneuvers that could respond to specific constraints encountered in different store locations and contexts.

▼▲ © Iwan Baan

The 20 m (65 ft) high façade wraps the existing building with a supple gradient of convex concrete panels.

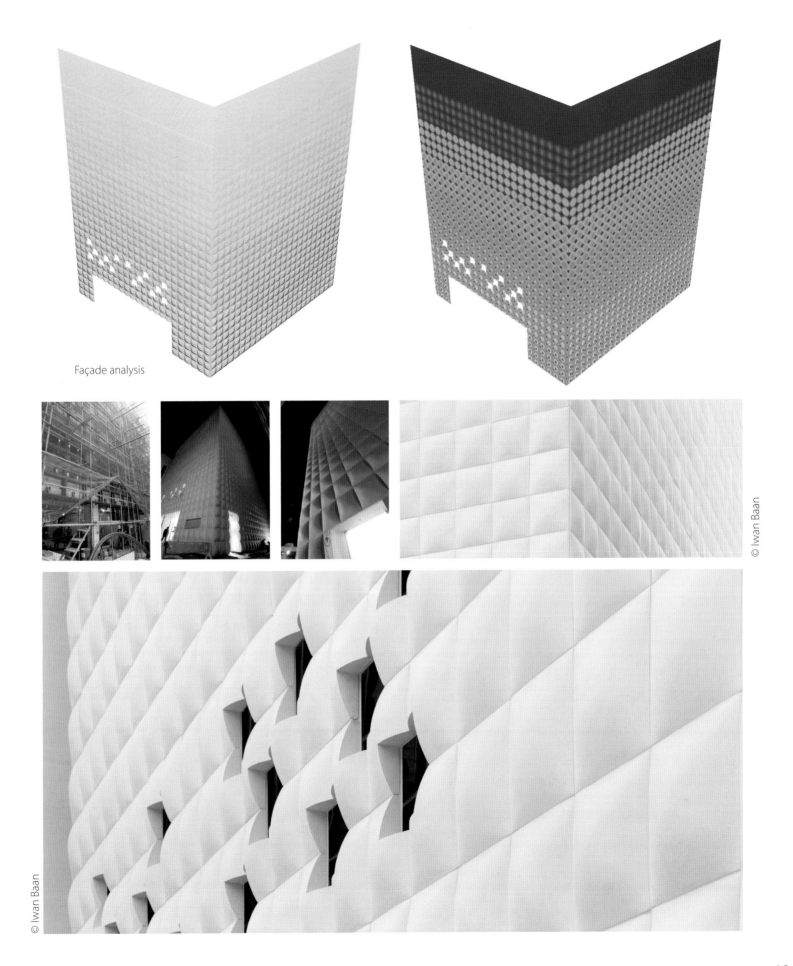

Façade analysis

© Iwan Baan

© Iwan Baan

Mass Studies - Minsuk Cho + Kisu Park

Ann Demeulemeester Shop

Seoul, South Korea   **Photographs:** Yong-Kwan Kim

The site is located in an alley, at a block's distance from Dosandae-ro – a busy thoroughfare in Seoul's Gangnam district – in close proximity to Dosan Park. Primarily residential in the past, the neighborhood is undergoing a rapid transformation into an upscale commercial district full of shops and restaurants. The building is comprised of one subterranean level and three floors above. The Ann Demeulemeester Shop is located on the first floor, with a restaurant above and a Multi-Shop in the basement. This proposal is an attempt to incorporate as much nature as possible into the building within the constraints of a low-elevation, high-density urban environment of limited space. The building defines its relationship between natural/artificial and interior/exterior as an amalgamation, rather than a confrontation. Diverse interior spaces designated for its three main programs were made to be perceived and utilized as a part of the outdoors in a variety of ways. This building is not meant to be just another 'object' to be experienced externally, but rather as a synthetic organism of nature and artifice. The parking lot/courtyard is at the center of the site, exposed to the street on the southern end. The entrance to the Ann Demeulemeester Shop is located on the western side of the courtyard, and stairs that lead to the other two programs are located on the eastern side. Landscaping of dense bamboo forms a wall along each of the remaining three sides that border neighboring sites. Inside the first floor shop, undulating dark brown exposed concrete forms an organically shaped ceiling. Round columns on the edges of the space continue the ceiling surface while providing the necessary structural support. This structural system creates arched openings of varying sizes that are open and as exposed as possible to the outside road and the bamboo hedges. This organic formation is not only a dynamic space but also a flexible rectangular one. The additional wing on the eastern side contains support functions such as fitting rooms, storage, and a bathroom, efficiently divided and connected at the same time. The outside building material is primarily a geotextile surface planted with a herbaceous perennial to form a living façade, while the other three sides that face the bamboo borders are clad in steel sheets and finished with propylene resin.

Architecture:
Mass Studies - Minsuk Cho + Kisu Park

23

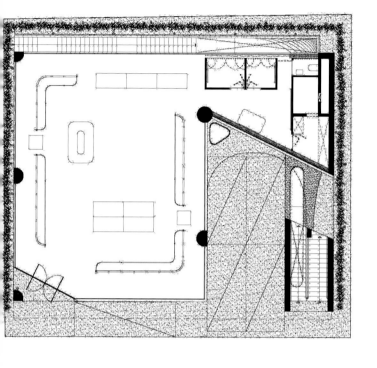

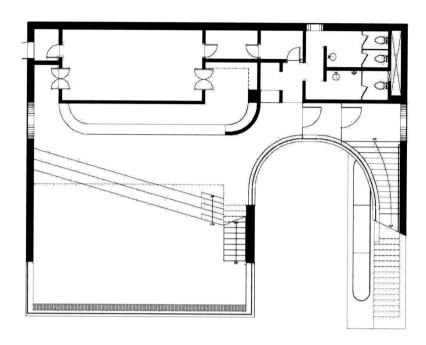

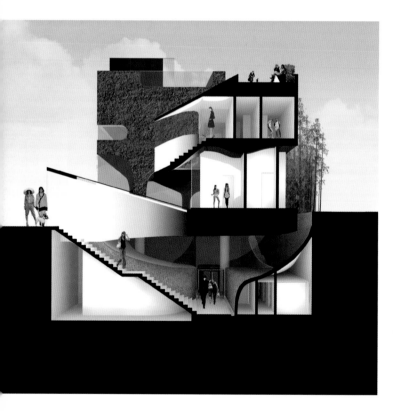

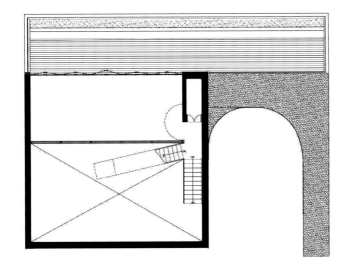

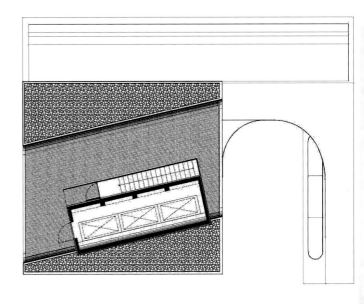

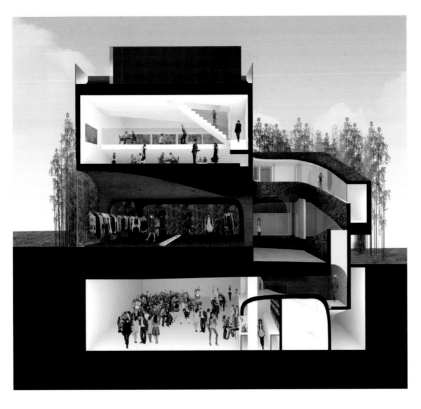

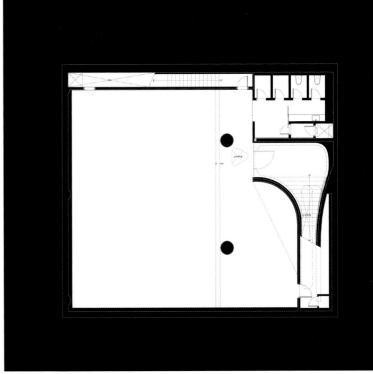

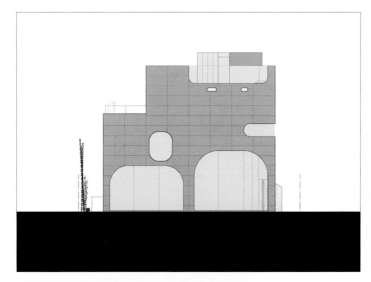

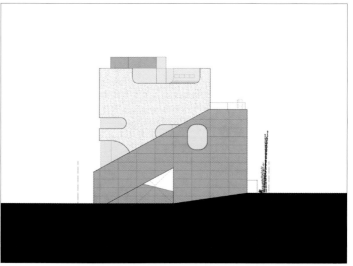

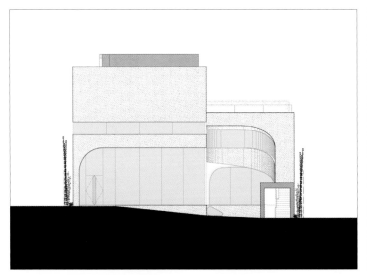

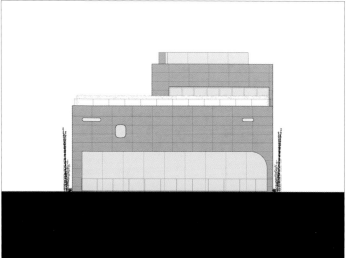

Office for Metropolitan Architecture (oma)

Prada New York Epicenter

New York City, USA

Photographs: Armin Linke, OMA & Prada

Prada's latest New York project is an interior conversion of the former Guggenheim store in Soho. The 2,100 sqm (23,000 sqft) are distributed between the ground floor and basement of the building.

A translucent wall of polycarbonate covers the existing brick wall of the building and establishes a dialogue between old and new. A mural of wallpaper on the entire length of the store allows for rapid change of the environment.

As a means to naturally connect to the basement and guide customers to the more invisible parts of the store, the floor steps downwards in its entire width and rises subsequently to re-connect to the ground level, creating a big 'wave'.

Located at the Broadway entrance, a round and fully glazed elevator displays bags and accessories. It descends into a lounge located underneath the wave, where the main dressing rooms are visible from display mattresses covered in techno gel that enable visitors to sit and watch people dress. The black-and-white marble floor is a reference to the first Prada store in Milan.

The northern part of the basement holds the archive, which is composed of 'movable walls', an adapted system of compact shelving that allows the sequence and size of spaces to be altered according to need. These Prada-green shelves contrast with the unfinished gypsum board walls and the wooden ceiling.

A series of experiential and service-oriented features enhances both the functioning and the ambience of the stores. The dressing rooms are equipped with 'magic mirrors': a plasma screen invisibly built into the large mirror surface that allows customers to see themselves both from the front and the back at the same time. An integrated time delay can even capture and replay movements.

The doors are made of Privalite glass that the customer can switch from transparent to translucent to control the privacy of the dressing room. Equipped with RFID [radio frequency identity] antennas, the 'garment closet' is able to register merchandize brought into the dressing room and display an inventory of icons on a touch screen. Here, the customer can request more specific information on the clothes, but also browse through alternative items of the collection.

Architecture:
Office for Metropolitan Architecture (oma)

Area:
2,100 sqm (23,000 sqft)

As a means to naturally connect to the basement and guide customers to the more invisible parts of the store, the floor steps downwards in its entire width and rises subsequently to re-connect to the ground level, creating a big 'wave'. The oversized stair made of zebra wood is used as an informal display space. At the push of a button, an event platform rotates out of the opposite part of the wave, turning the stair into an auditorium for performances, film projections and lectures.

Site plan

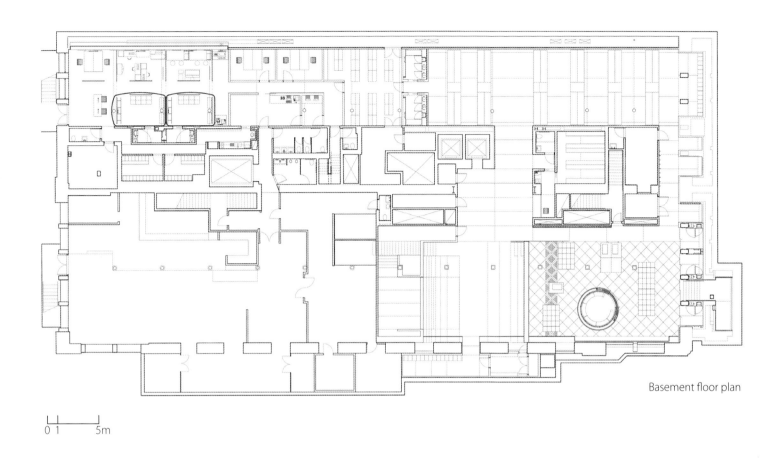

Basement floor plan

0 1 5m

Ground floor plan

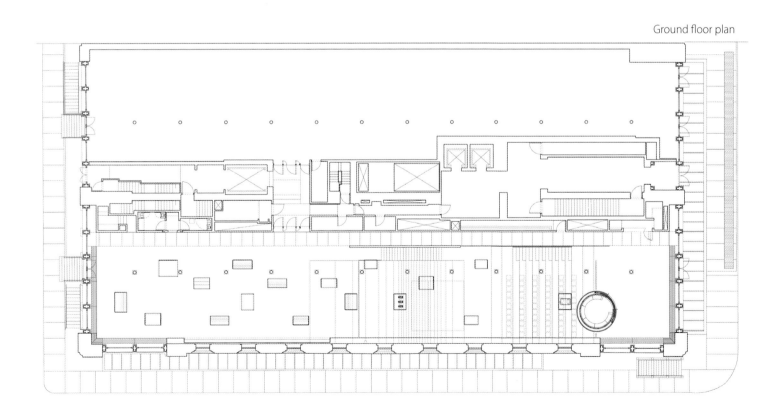

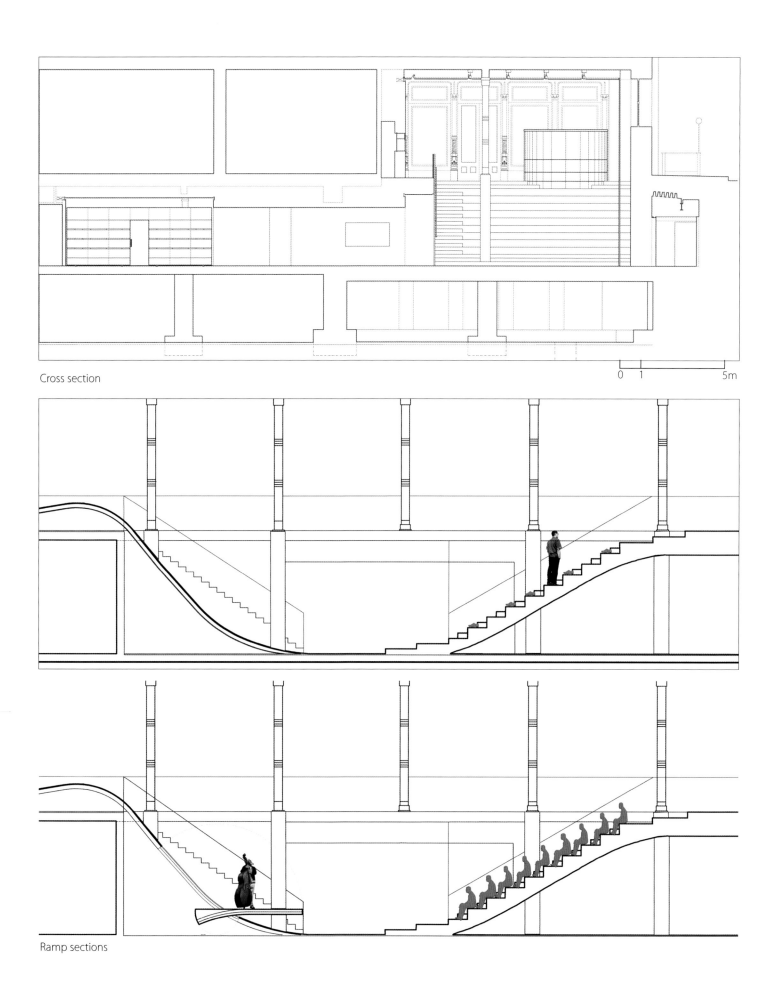

Cross section

0 1   5m

Ramp sections

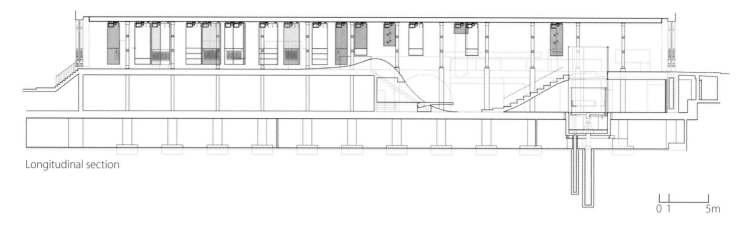

Longitudinal section

0 1   5m

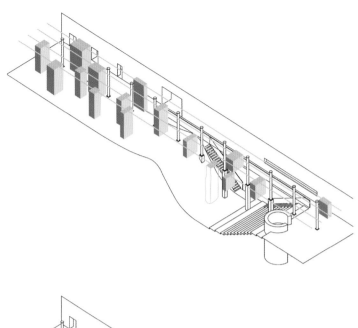

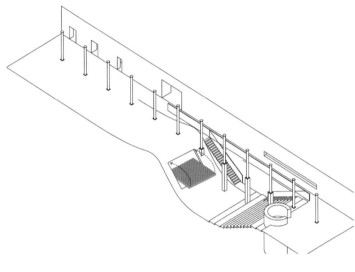

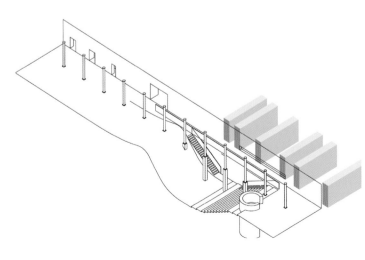

The merchandise throughout the ground floor is displayed in moveable volumes. This "hanging city" consists of a series of aluminum-mesh cages suspended from the ceiling which are configured to include hanging bars, shelving, and space for mannequins. The units are mounted on motorized tracks for flexibility. During events on the wave stage, the hanging city can be gathered together in a concentrated block at the back of the store.

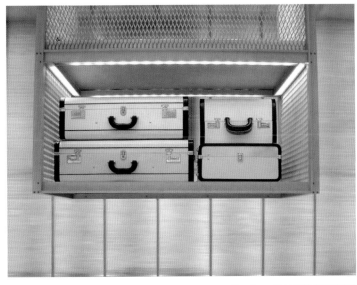

Muti Randolph

Galeria Melissa

Sao Paulo, Brazil

Photographs: Romulo Fialdini

Architecture:
Muti Randolph

Plastic.o.rama made in Brazil, is a project that arose under the auspices of Melissa, a major plastics producer that recently celebrated its 25th birthday.

Famous for the "Hawaianas" rubber sandals that have invaded the world, Melissa has become an effective worldwide representative of Made in Brazil, Melissa creates fashion accessories in plastic, especially footwear. The enterprise has commissioned renowned personalities in the worlds of fashion and design (Fernando & Umberto Campana and Karim Rashid, among others), to generate a colorful, fantastic world of plastic, a sort of ethical Disneyland for design accessory fans.

The setting for the collection, Galeria Melissa, is also a hymn to plastics. Muti Randolph has utilized plastics in all possible expressive ways. (...) The footwear in bright colors is contained in transparent bubbles that emerge from something similar to shiny horns-of-plenty. The unusual display system features clusters of these elements that descend from the ceiling or wrap themselves around bases rising from the floor, moulded in shiny white plastic.

There are also biological connotations: the display fixtures look disturbingly like large spermatozoa. The sinuous pattern of the stripes, an effective op reference, produces psychedelic sensations. The recessed volume, off-axis with respect to the street, leaves a polygonal plaza underlined by a bright yellow base and a sky blue tympanum. This space can be used for outdoor events. The perspective device gives the façade the role of a flag (striped) visible from a distance.

Not just a boutique but also an exhibition space, Galeria Melissa hosts seasonal art installations in its plastic garden. In the spring of 2005 (our autumn) the green stems brandished large colored buds. Because the very evident aim is to astonish, the setting changes with each season, including new furnishings created by the imaginative Muti Randolph, making Galeria Melissa a space in a continuous state of mutation.

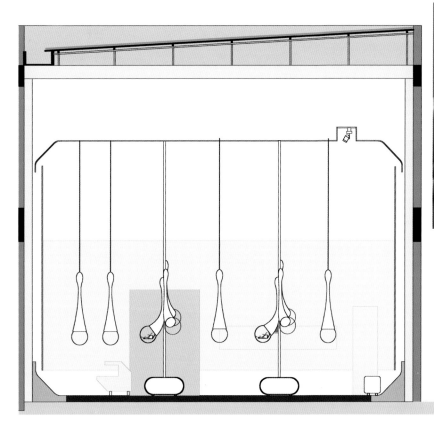

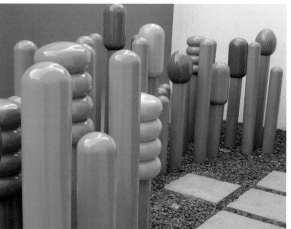

Cross section D

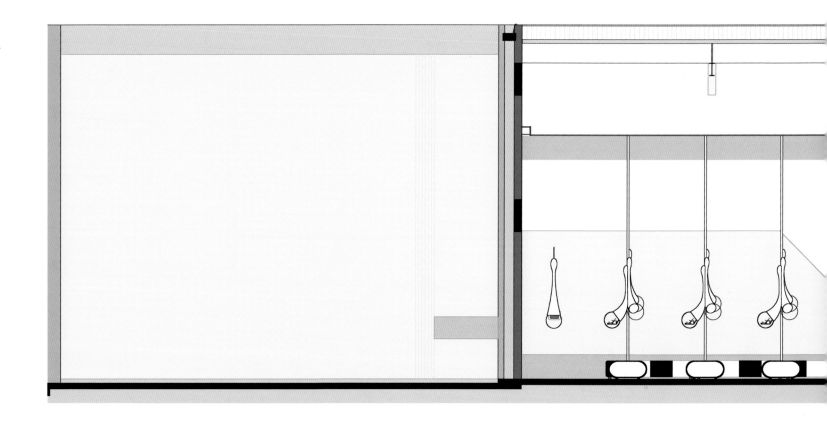

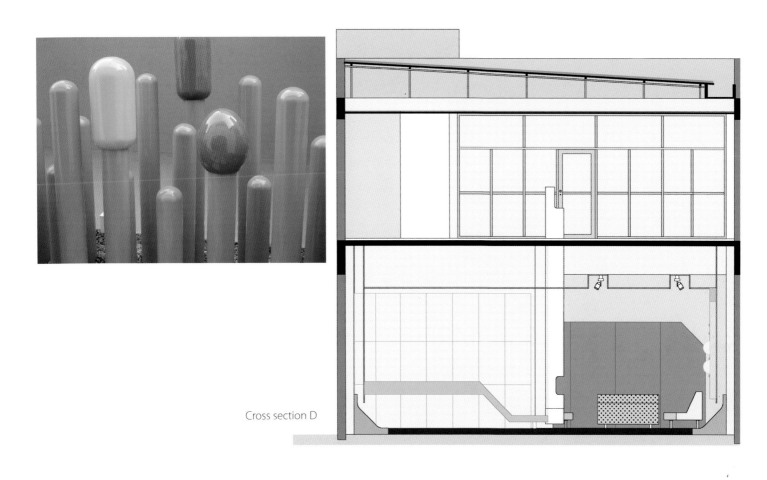

Cross section D

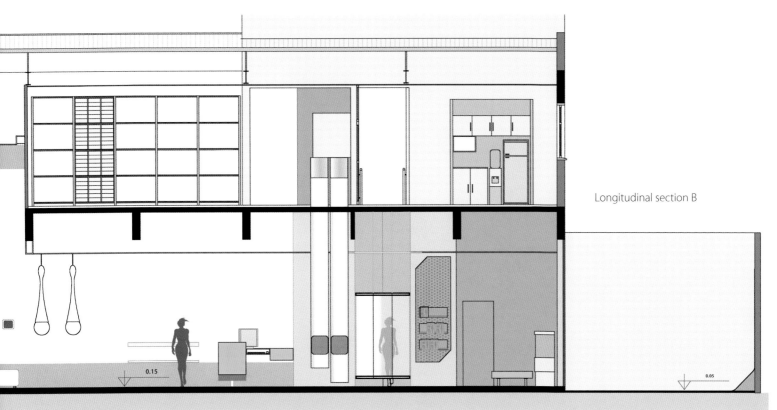

Longitudinal section B

0.15

0.05

The sinuous pattern of the stripes, an effective op reference, produces psychedelic sensations. The recessed volume, off-axis with respect to the street, leaves a polygonal plaza underlined by a bright yellow base and a sky blue tympanum. This space can be used for outdoor events. The perspective device gives the façade the role of a flag (striped) visible from a distance.

ArchLAB - Antonio Pio Saracino + Steve E. Blatz Architects

Tibi

New York, USA   **Photographs:** Adrian Wilson

Tibi is a contemporary women's-wear boutique located in SOHO, NYC. Known for their 70's inspired bold print textiles, Tibi challenged ArchLAB to develop a brand identity that made a strong statement reflecting the essence of the brand for their first free-standing retail boutique.

The architecture of this 200 sqm (2,200 sqft) sales space is inspired by the decorative prints emblematic of the client's work. The architects, principals Antonio P io Saracino and Steve E.Blatz, transformed the prints into two folded canopies hovering within the typical SOHO white box. The sculpted forms of the canopies create an entrance arch visible from the storefront window that draws shoppers into the space. The front canopy floats above the floor, folds down along the side wall, incorporates the cash desk and swoops back up towards the ceiling creating an illusionary perspective sense of movement into the space. Together, the two canopies divide the shop into four distinct shopping zones and bring an intimacy to the over-scaled ceilings of the box. The canopies are hand-painted with thick layers of acrylic paint in a floral design evocative of the artisan nature of both the architecture and the client's collection. The black and green motif developed by the architects uses the signature colors of the client's brand. The hand-painted canopies, with their decorative motif, were conceived to wrap around the shopper to create a playful architectural experience.

A facetted pale green display wall floats along one wall of the boutique and wraps itself around the stairs to the lower level that houses the pattern room. The facetted wall forms a children's play area near the rear dressing rooms so that mothers may shop undistracted from their children.

Large fitting rooms wrapped in white drapes in a custom steel structure sit at the back of the boutique below a full width skylight that brings natural light to the changing rooms. The fitting rooms include custom lighting designed by the architects. Minimalist custom designed blackened steel display fixtures form a simple backdrop to Tibi's products.

Architecture:
ArchLAB -
Antonio Pio Saracino +
Steve E. Blatz Architects

Area:
200 sqm (2,200 sqft)

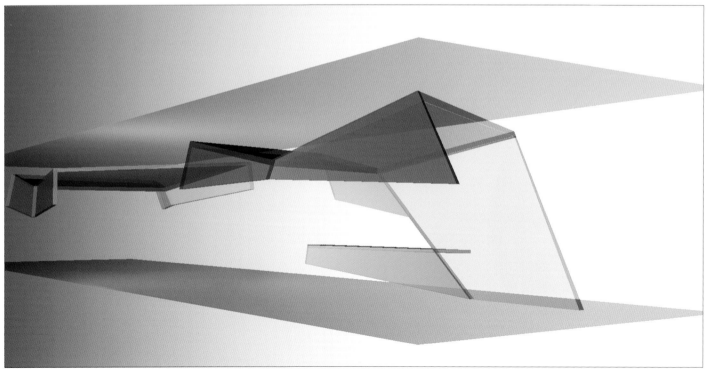

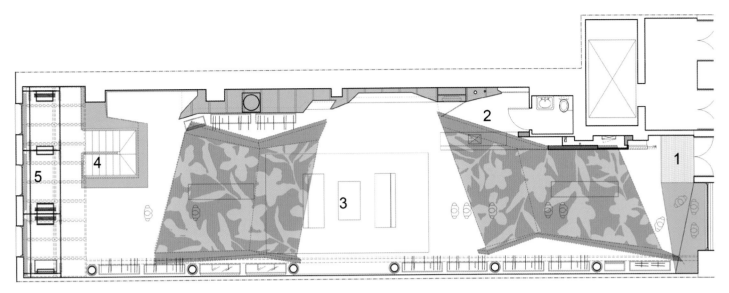

1. Entrance
2. Cash wrap
3. Living room
4. Stair
5. Fitting room

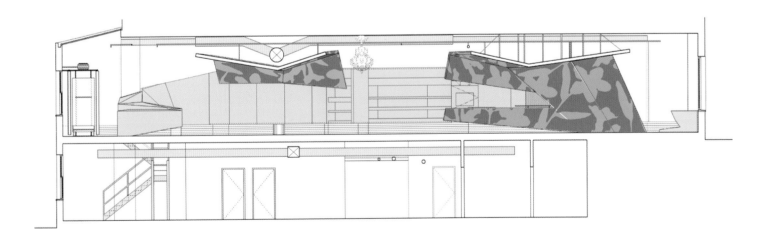

In order to connect the shop with Soho's history as a home to artists and galleries an artist was selected to hand paint the pattern onto the thickly-texturd canopies in Tibi's signature colors.

Hiroshi Nakamura & NAP Associates

Lanvin Boutique Ginza

Tokyo, Japan   **Photographs:** contributed by the architects

Architecture:
Hiroshi Nakamura & NAP Associates

The guiding concept behind the design scheme was that of thousands of photons which are constantly shifting. They change their surroundings, which in this case are made up of sunlight, street-life and the interior of the space. Cloaked in these photons, the building is meant to sparkle like a diamond and cast shards of light on its surroundings.

Located in Ginza Central Street (one of the busiest fashion districts in downtown Tokyo), this Lanvin boutique is the flagship store of a French line of clothing. The design of the shop was inspired by the sort of contemporary French residence where modern and classical elements meet. For example, the façade consists of a continuous steel plate with 3000 clear acrylic cylinders inserted as tiny windows, emulating the look of a Lanvin diamond-embroidered party dress.

While frames, sealants, and many other materials for window detailing are typically used, it was decided in this case that any ordinary details would ruin the subtle yet rich phenomenon that the ephemeral light creates right at each opening. Borrowing from the craft of boat building, the designers invented 'hiyashi hame', a method to avoid having any obstructions at the window's edge, aiming to turn the openings into something more than simple windows (in fact, they are now applying for the patent). The desired effect was to turn them into photons.

The literal meaning of 'hiyashi hame' is 'cooling insert' and it is now the newest window detail in the world. First acrylic cylinders are pre-frozen to shrink the acrylic. These cylinders are then inserted into holes that have been punched in the steel plate. As they warm to room temperature, they expand are thus held without any frames or adhesives. The end result is a very natural and gentle façade that reflects and diffuses light, creating limitless photons. By containing these photons, the plain steel wall now generates a complex and rich phenomenon inside and outside of the shop.

1. Acrylic cylinders have been chosen because the acrylic expands equally in all directions as it warms.

2. Steel sleeves for the cylinders are sandwiched between steel plates.

To create the new window detail, acrylic cylinders were shrunk via freezing and then inserted into holes in a metal wall. As the cylinders warm to room temperature, they expand and are thus permanently fixed within the wall structure.

3. After freezing the acrylic cylinders, they are transported to the construction site.

4. The acrylic cylinders are inserted into the steel wall.

5. Finally, the cylinders gradually unthaw to room temperature and the process is complete.

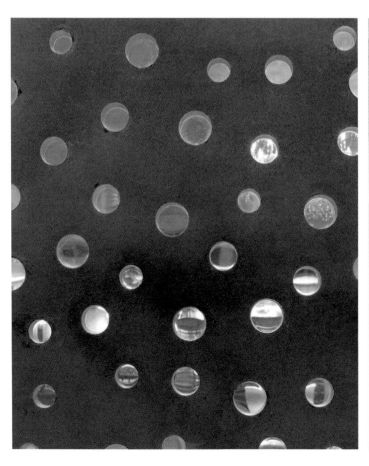

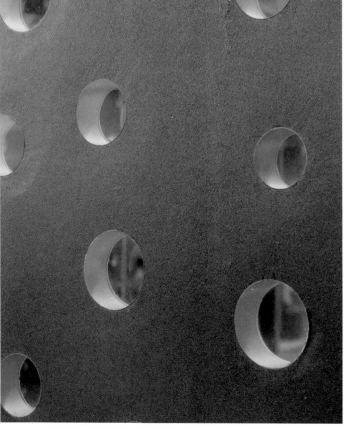

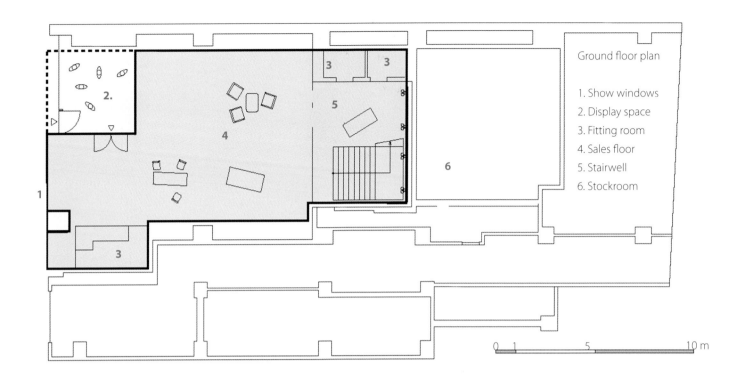

Ground floor plan

1. Show windows
2. Display space
3. Fitting room
4. Sales floor
5. Stairwell
6. Stockroom

0 1   5   10 m

First floor plan

1. Sales floor
2. Tailoring room
3. Fitting room
4. VIP Salon
5. Atelier
6. Stockroom

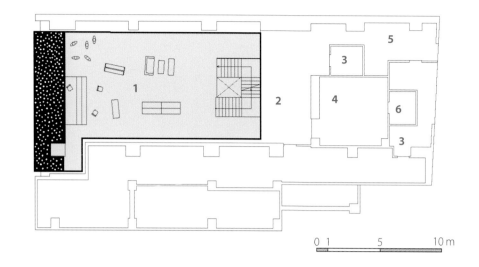

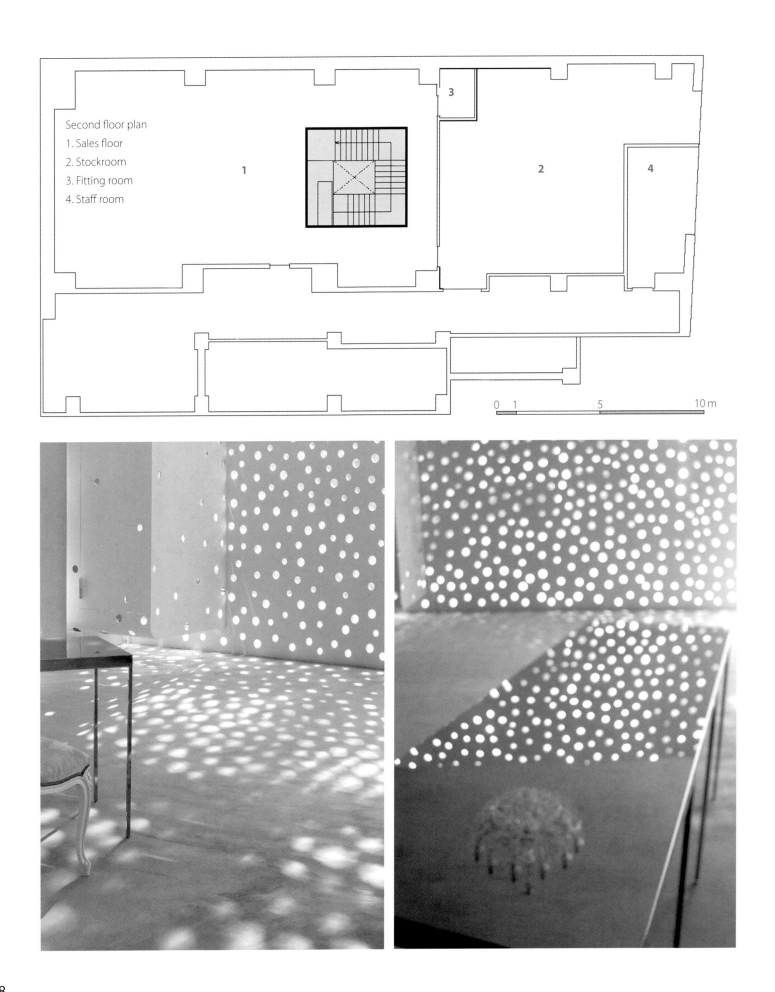

Second floor plan
1. Sales floor
2. Stockroom
3. Fitting room
4. Staff room

0 1   5   10 m

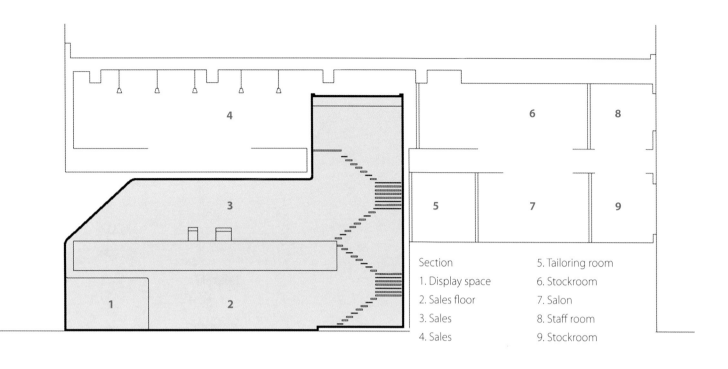

Section

1. Display space	5. Tailoring room
2. Sales floor	6. Stockroom
3. Sales	7. Salon
4. Sales	8. Staff room
	9. Stockroom

Universal Design Studio

Franqueensense

Aoyama, Tokyo, Japan

Photographs: contributed by Universal Design Studio

Universal Design Studio is recognized as one of the world's most innovative creative design consultancies. The firm's multi-disciplinary approach towards the design of branded environments creates unique, arresting, comprehensive environments with effective commercial purpose. The studio was commissioned to design the first flagship store for United Arrows' new womenswear brand, Franqueensense, in Tokyo's fashionable shopping district Aoyama.

Universal Design Studio's concept articulated the brand value of 'approachable luxury' as two distinct environments to create a unique, unified store. These two environments support the brand's two complementary fashion collections, 'Precious' and 'Easy'.

The Precious environment is defined by a floating screen of circular lenses. This screen has been conceived as a modern interpretation of the chandelier and delicately refracts light and generates shifting views of the merchandise, the customers and the surrounding Aoyama street scenes. It has been applied throughout the store serving as a partition wall between the different clothing ranges, defining circulation routes and accompanying the handrail on the spiral staircase, and thereby establishing a dialogue with the upper floor. The small acrylic disks that comprise its structure animate the store through their subtle movements, lending a kinetic and delicate character to its interior. The screen has since become a strong and recognizable identity for the Franqueensense brand.

The material palette of the Precious area imbues a luxurious feel through polished brass, soft carpets in dusky pink hues, polished marble and brightly anodized aluminum.

The Easy area is a simpler and more informal space inspired by the modern salon. A series of deliberately relaxed materials have been used to challenge the magical elegance of the Precious area. The walls and furniture are mainly white and reflect a more functional aesthetic. The flooring is walnut board, edged with a brass trim where it meets the carpeted shapes of the Precious zone.

Architecture:
Universal Design Studio

Team:
Jenny Jones, Sonia Tomic, David Card, Celia Richardson, Nick Rolls

Lighting concept:
Gary Campbell of DPA lighting

Project management:
Nanno Junji of Hip

Client:
Perennial United Arrows

Total floor area:
3,300 sqft (300 sqm)

Universal Design Studio's concept articulated the brand value of 'approachable luxury' as two distinct environments to create a unique, unified store.

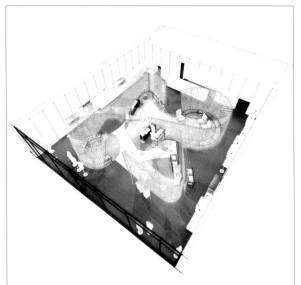

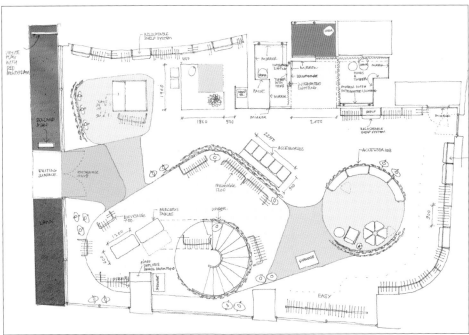

The Precious area is defined by curtains of sparkling acrylic disks that generate a magical aesthetic, refracting the light and imbuing the space with a sense of motion.

Matteo Thun

Hugo Boss

New York, USA

Photographs: Paul Warchol

In the heart of a neighborhood which used to be the commercial epicenter of meatpacking, the new Hugo Boss store is a seamless blend of rough urban surfaces with the texture of contemporary art, interacting with nearby Chelsea, concrete, iron and electricity.

Concrete penetrates the floors, provides a finishing touch for the walls together with exposed brickwork, and can then be found on the ceiling, where it is painted black and blends with the metal of the electrical and mechanical conduits and the pattern of adjustable industrial spotlights. This is the store's shell, and it fits in neatly with the spirit of the place.

On the inside, Hugo Boss brings its four BOSS lines (BOSS Black, BOSS Orange, BOSS Selection and BOSS Green) and the HUGO brand together to create a 'total look' providing a complete and simultaneous brand experience, displaying its own distinctive signs on various levels: from the well-established retail system to the structure made of diamond-shaped wooden panels, the distinctive iconic architectural element from the Coldrerio offices in Milan.

The interior is divided into two parts: the first part serves as a display space, where the burnished iron and dark brown lacquered displays for the various collections, and the leather and glass showcases for the accessories are all located. A Corian counter offers shoppers refreshments against the backdrop of a metal wall. The area also modulates the hangers, racks and goods against spots on the floor and the diamond-shaped sections of the wooden structure. A reflective "focus wall" at the back marks the boundaries of this section and plays with the sense of perspective.

The second part can be seen in semi-transparency and plays host to the fitting rooms. The atmosphere is softer and warmer, featuring rugs, red velvet curtains, a golden colored ceiling and wooden elements. Designed in conjunction with American light designer AJ Weissbard, the lighting mechanism in the display area is extremely intricate. Dynamic light is provided by programmable LEDs against the pattern of perimeter panels, which runs along the concrete and exposed brick walls. The light display is toned down in the fitting rooms, where only indirect lighting is used with the exception of a number of candelabras.

Architecture:
Matteo Thun

Project manager:
Michael Catoir

Team:
Sabrina Pinkes, Anna Worzewski

Total building area:
4,040 sqft (375 sqm)

existing
canopy structure

Frontal façade

The interior is divided into two parts: the first part serves as a display space, where the burnished iron and dark brown lacquered displays for the various collections, and the leather and glass showcases for the accessories are all located.

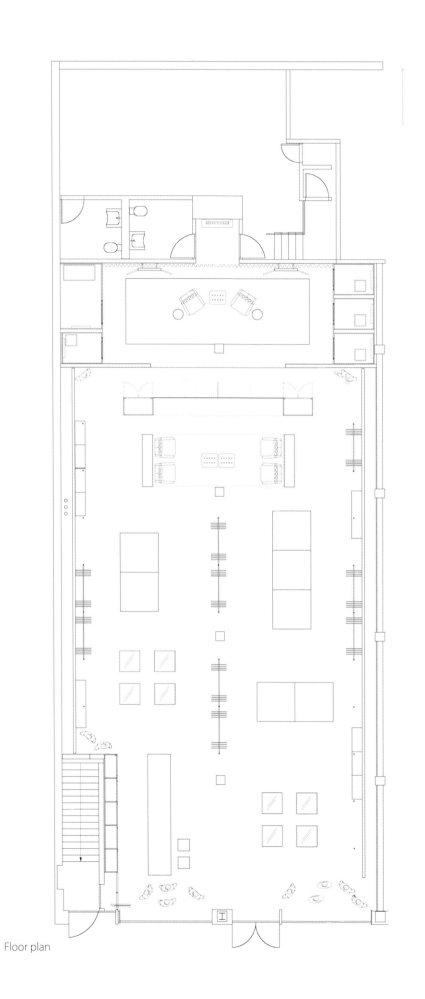

Floor plan

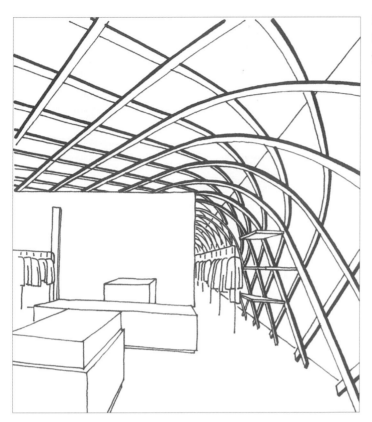

Light plays a fundamental role throughout, tracing the twin spirit of the Hugo Boss store: solid and urban along the road and intimate and private further back, but always interacting with the city.

Sybarite

Stefanel New Concept

Frankfurt, Germany

Photographs: Marco Zanta

This Frankfurt flagship is the first installment of Sybarite's new shop concept for Stefanel. Part of a complete rebranding effort, the concept is a modern and stylized solution, designed to propel this Italian knitwear label in a completely new direction and firmly into the future of retail.

The brief was to create a completely new image for Stefanel shops, a strong and recognizable architectural language that would become synonymous with their brand identity. With rollout plans for 700 locations worldwide – from large flagships to tiny shop-in-shops – the concept had to offer exceptional value for money, ease of installation and adaptability to widely varying sites. The result is a modular system which achieves complete flexibility without sacrificing aesthetics or imagination. Lending itself to repetition and variation as a method of building composition, the final outcome can grow organically in response to a particular site and evolve over time in collaboration with the client. The components, mainly gloss lacquered GRP and polished stainless steel, are fabricated off site and come together fluidly to form the walls, display surfaces and furniture, creating the impression of a continuous form molded into display props and surfaces. The sense of composition is reinforced by the attention paid to the smallest detail. The motif of square into circle repeats throughout, from the curvy rectangles of the wall units and freestanding furniture to the bespoke stools, shelves and door handles. The language is incorporated into stylized mannequins and hangers and is echoed in the minimalism of the window vitrines.

The starting point of the design was to address the particular challenges faced by Stefanel. For example, Stefanel's complicated knitwear designs don't display to their full potential on standard mannequins, or even stay on them properly. The solution was a bespoke design contoured with flocking material, which holds the garments in place and brings their detailing into view. By providing non-slip functionality in such a graphic and recognizable way, a display prop moves beyond its obvious functionality to enhance brand identity.

The design provides the client with complete flexibility and future expandability. Every surface offers a means of display, which can be as dense or as sparse as necessary. Merchandising can change by season or collection and the system's modularity easily permits both the addition of extra components and the development of new ones, ensuring the concept can adapt to meet future needs and evolve along with Stefanel.

Architecture:
Sybarite

Client:
Stefanel

Specialist Fabricator:
Soozar

Part of a complete rebranding effort, the concept is a modern and stylized solution, designed to propel this Italian knitwear label in a completely new direction and firmly into the future of retail.

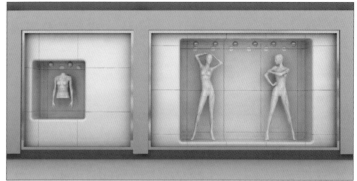

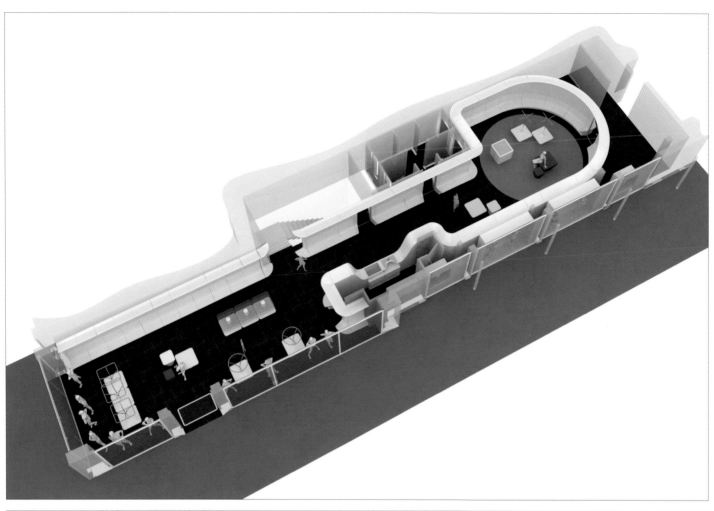

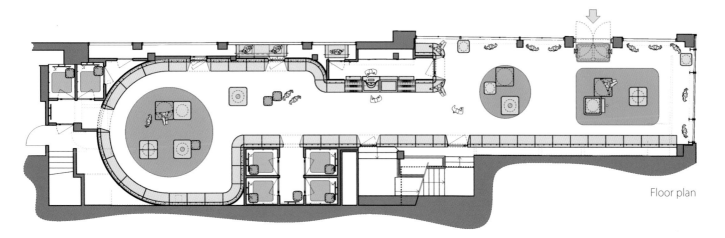

Floor plan

Lending itself to repetition and variation as a method of building composition, the final outcome can grow organically in response to a particular site and evolve over time in collaboration with the client.

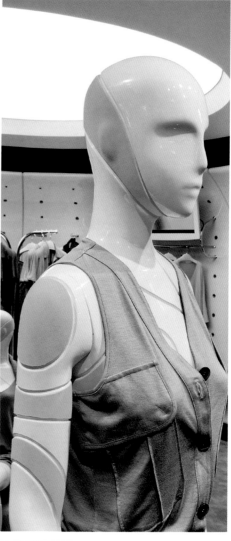

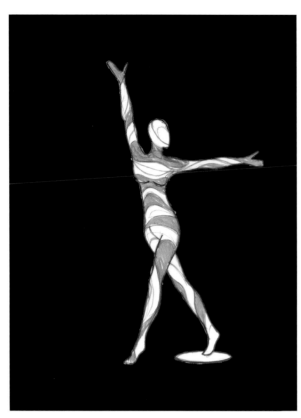

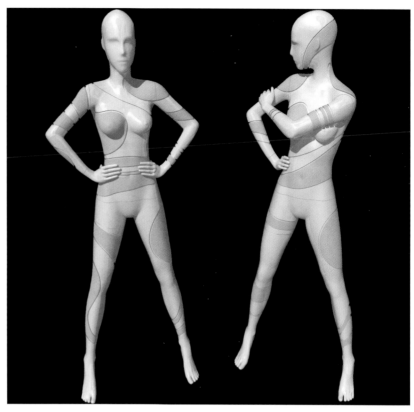

Raiser Lopes Designers

Boss Orange

Shanghai, China

Photographs: Martin Grothmaak

The Boss Orange store in Shanghai has been individually designed by Raiser Lopes Designers, who have been responsible for many of this fashion retailer's stores around the world. Simple and economic materials dominate the interior architecture of this shop to create an experimental ambience of modesty and honesty. The ground floor offers two possible access points. This 65 sqm (700 sqft) surface area introduces the visitor to the first floor. The "Fashion box" containing some of the stars from the latest collections generates curiosity and offers the customer a taste of what's to come. This floor is a simple "introductory" space and contains just a few simple display stands with an oiled wooden finish. The stairs that lead to the first floor are fitted with banisters made from wire netting. Two more fashion boxes await customers here along with an integrated changing room and a lounge area furnished with antique pieces. Hanging racks provide a frame for this room, which houses the most part of the store's collection. The details in the furniture and on the walls, combined with the raggedness and a certain individuality, transport the image of the street into the store's interior The Furniture, fashion-boxes and shop system were especially developed for the store. The boxes are slightly raised, and so a small step has been provided to facilitate their access. These boxes, which are for both men and women, have not been designed to be moved. Each one generates its own space, allowing customers to feel as if they have a "mini-shop" to themselves. The boxes facilitate the definition of different zones within the boundaries of the store. Lounge areas and functional areas can intermingle without causing any kind of confusion. Furthermore the functional layout of the floor plan can be altered and upgraded by modifying the interior of one or more of these spaces. Hand painted illustrations on the walls and furnishings and the locally plaited handrail help to make every part of the shop unique and original. The store concept creates tension between inside and outside enabling a wide range of unexpected, surprising elements, which stimulate the customers. The regeneration of an old style is reinterpreted here to create an open, eclectic and unpredictable interior.

Architecture:
Raiser Lopes Designers

Area:
265 sqm (2,900 sqft)

The "Fashion box" containing some of the stars from the latest collections generates curiosity and offers the customer a taste of what's to come.

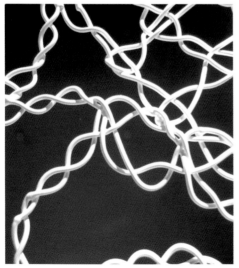

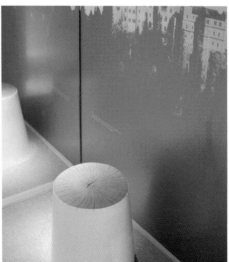

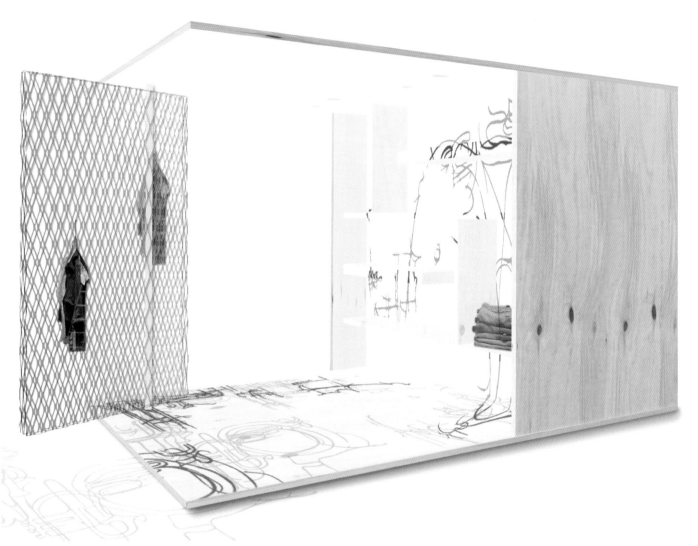

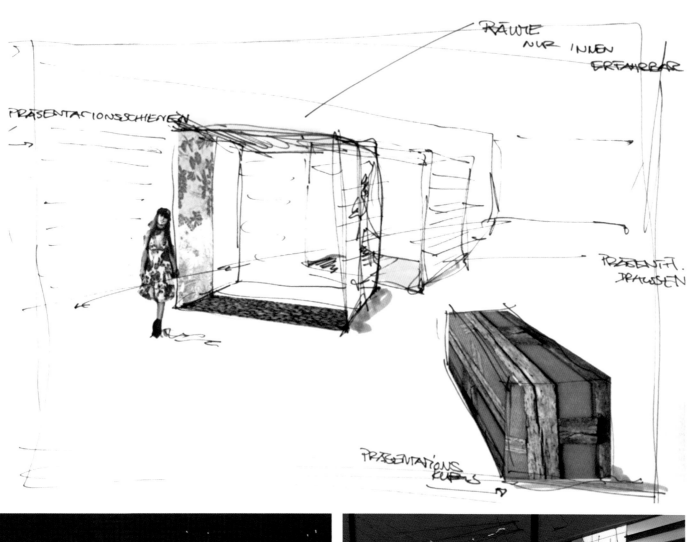

RÄUME
NUR INNEN
ERFAHRBAR

PRÄSENTATIONSSCHIENEN

PRÄSENTT.
DRAUSSEN

PRÄSENTATIONS
KUBUS

Peter Marino, FAIA

Fendi Roma

Rome, Italy   **Photographs:** Matteo Piazza

This flagship store in Rome represents the re-launch of a luxury brand. The architect sought a store concept which would emphasize the brand's Roman identity both in a local sense as well as in an universal sense of Rome as caput mundi. Rome is identified as material essences: travertine and the basalt cobble stones called sampietrini. Travertine is perceived in tactile and visual terms as horizontal striations. The rust encrustations often found on the surfaces of Roman fountains presented another essence. The striations of travertine become the point of departure for variations on the theme as irregular ribbing of surfaces encrusted in rust, basalt, amber glass. The store's urban placement in Largo Goldoni places it along the central axis of the Tridente which framed urban development in Rome and also at the intersection of another axis leading to the Spanish Steps (via dei Condotti). In such a context the Baroque became a critical reference for the brand identity. It is less an historical reference than it is an association based on architectural and phenomenological meaning in terms in movement through space, multiple vantage points, linear and spatial complexity, infinity, technological speculation, and multiplicity of materials. The store becomes an interiorization of Roma barocca. The passage from the portone of via Fontanella Borghese carries the street paving of sampietrini inside as in Nolli's map, which defines courtyards as negative space equivalent to the street. The store has multiple entrances that offer routes through which the pedestrian can access the various passages and rooms of the store, and which occupies two floors of the palazzo. Yellow travertine becomes a flat wall surface as it does a curvilinear valance floating above the merchandise racks. In the fur salons rust encrusted striations serve as walls below the travertine curves while handbags float on Thasos shelves and in niches cut into the yellow travertine. Here white striated curves float above the goods. Shoes rest on travertine planes floating below curved travertine curtains. The dark gray metallic restoration of the neoclassical stair becomes a counterpoint to the chromatic richness of the store interiors.

Architecture:
Peter Marino, FAIA

Ground floor plan
1. Arcade
2. Court
3. Women's shoes
4. Women's bags
5. Women's sunglasses
6. Women's watches
7. Stair
8. Stock

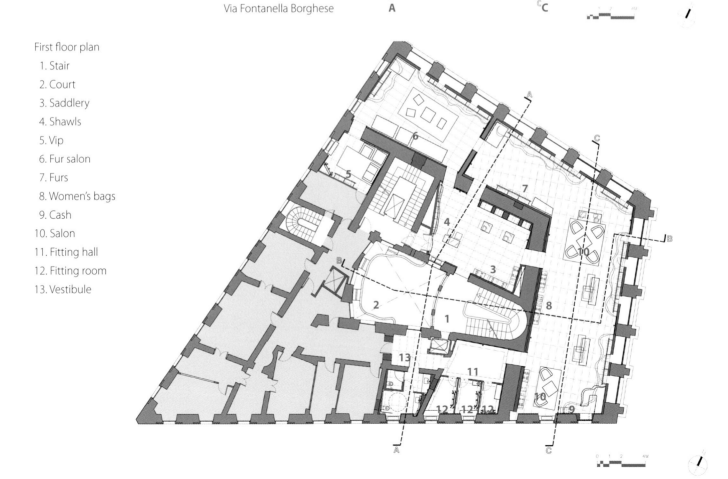

First floor plan
1. Stair
2. Court
3. Saddlery
4. Shawls
5. Vip
6. Fur salon
7. Furs
8. Women's bags
9. Cash
10. Salon
11. Fitting hall
12. Fitting room
13. Vestibule

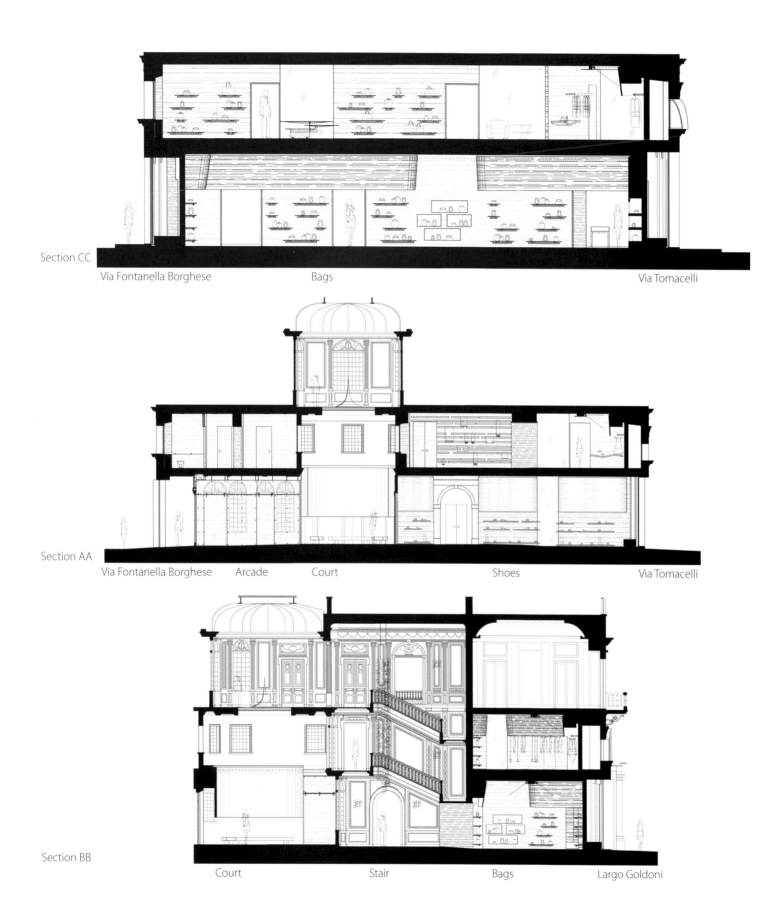

Section CC

Via Fontanella Borghese   Bags   Via Tomacelli

Section AA

Via Fontanella Borghese   Arcade   Court   Shoes   Via Tomacelli

Section BB

Court   Stair   Bags   Largo Goldoni

113

Façade elevation

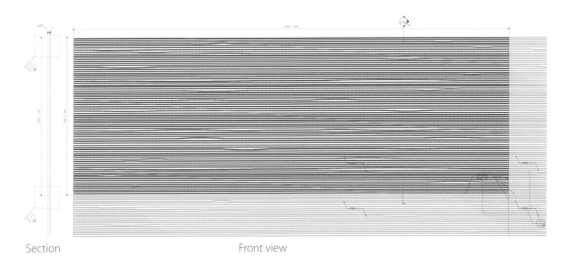

Section   Front view

Ribbed wood panel

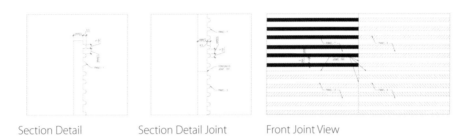

Section Detail   Section Detail Joint   Front Joint View

Dear design

Lurdes Bergada, Syngman Cucala

Barcelona, Spain

Photographs: Pol Cucala

Ignasi Llauradó and Eric Dufourd, the founders of the Barcelona-based design and architecture studio Dear design were commissioned to design a new flagship store for Lurdes Bergada, Syngman Cucala, in one of Barcelona's major shopping centers, L'Illa Diagonal. With this project Dear design continues its own exploration into novel design concepts and original architectural codes in the world of retail. The store is divided into two clearly defined areas which, on the one hand, link all technical aspects of a clothes store behind a 'wooden skin'; and on the other, maintain the clothes as the main focus. The project seeks to preserve the common characteristics of Lurdes Bergada, Syngman Cucala's existing spaces, which are industrial, original and minimalist, and incorporate a touch of the contemporary in their architecture. The basic idea was to open the space and allow views over the shopping center's park. This would give clients the sensation of shopping in a space full of natural light, as though they were in a street store. With this concept, Deardesign applied the mall's central philosophy: a shopping center that feels more like a shopping high street. The park is another decorative piece of the interior, and offers shoppers clear views of the back façade, which is used to attract clients in the same way as the mall's interior façade.

The design team decided to bring together all the technical functions of the store (storage, fitting rooms, electrical services, and a second smaller window) in a huge unique structure made from 1,000 pieces of wood and put together with 2,400 screws. The wooden skin allows all large structures to be hidden, thereby leaving the roof clear. From it's interior, the 'skin' reveals all it's technical, constructive secrets, bringing to mind fabric, turn-ups, stitching, etc... This reflects the importance of technology in clothes making and enhances the concepts transmitted by the brand: simplicity, purity, and industry. The installation, pieced together from irregular triangles, appears rocklike, a contemporary cave. The natural beech wood forms a contrast with the opposite wall, made of concrete. Each triangle is unique and numbered to make the construction easier.

Basic materials such as concrete for the walls and fine cement on the floor are used. These simple materials simplify the architectural reading of the store and strengthen the concept.

Architecture:
Dear design

Design Team:
Ignasi Llauradó,
Eric Dufourd,
Dorien Peeters

Consultant:
Xyloformas

Client:
Lurdes Bregada,
Syngman Cucala

Most of the brand's existing stores preserve traces of the history of the buildings in which they are installed. The aim of this project was to respect the original context and to reinforce the industrial characteristics of the building.

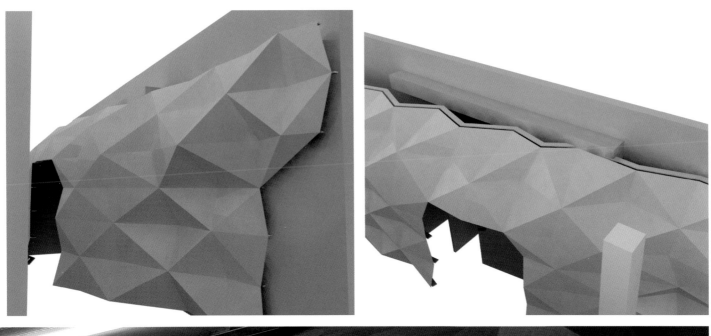

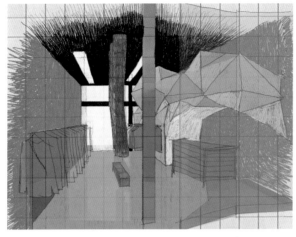

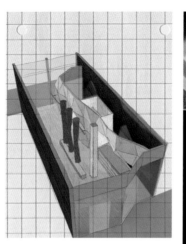

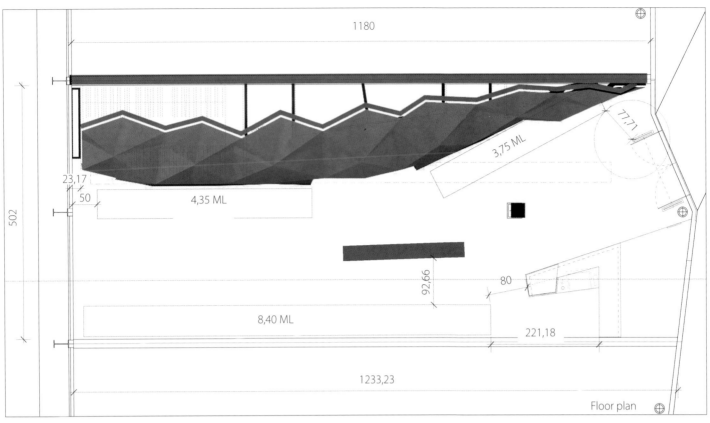

1180

502

23,17

50

4,35 ML

3,75 ML

77,71

92,66

80

8,40 ML

221,18

1233,23

Floor plan

124

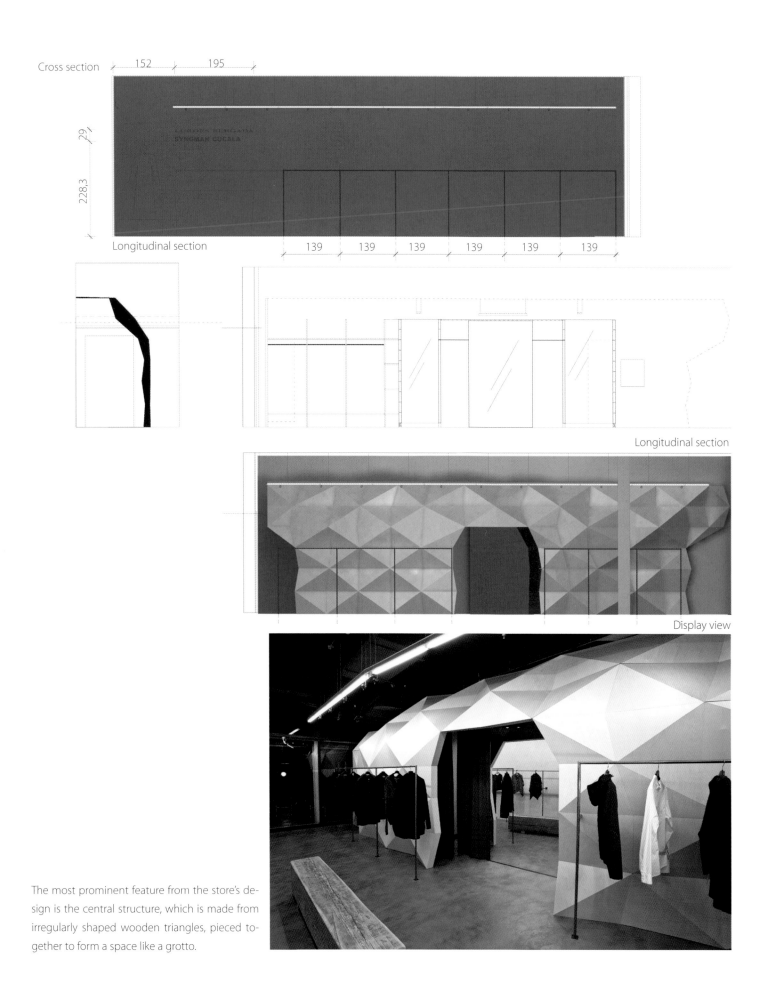

Cross section

152   195

29

228,3

Longitudinal section   139   139   139   139   139   139

Longitudinal section

Display view

The most prominent feature from the store's design is the central structure, which is made from irregularly shaped wooden triangles, pieced together to form a space like a grotto.

Sinato

Patrick Cox

Tokyo, Japan

Photographs: Toshiyuki Yano

Patrick Cox is an eponymous fashion label specializing in the creation of shoes, leather goods and accessories. Cox is most noted for the use of unusual materials and a mixture of avant-garde and traditional styles. For its store in Tokyo's fashion-centric Aoyama, the brand commissioned Japanese architecture and design studio Sinato, headed by architect Chikara Ohno, to develop an interior design concept that would highlight the exclusive nature of the products on sale. The store is housed within a building that rises to 17 stories in total, and is located very close to the main entrance.

One of the key elements on which the design capitalizes is the lighting. Since the products are, generally speaking, small in nature and in order to allow customers to be able to examine them in detail and admire the craftsmanship, it was decided to have the light source close by. For this reason there are no ceiling lights. In fact all the lights are concentric cylindrical steel pendant fixtures that hang down from the ceiling, directly over a corresponding display pedestal.

The result of this unique lighting system is an environment in which anything above the cylinders, roughly set at head height, is kept in darkness, while anything below is very clearly illuminated. This focused lighting, together with the circular platforms, creates the sensation that the items on display are the leading characters on a stage.

White dominates as a finish throughout the shop, increasing the focus on the products and reflecting the light and enhancing the shadows. Shelves along the back wall are also lit with the same pure white lighting. The display pedestals have been carefully arranged so that customers can easily move among them.

Architecture:
Sinato

Designer:
Chikara Ohno

Client:
BLBG Co., Ltd.

Floor area:
850 sqft (79 sqm)

The simplicity of the display architecture, both in form and in color, allows the high quality product range to speak for itself.

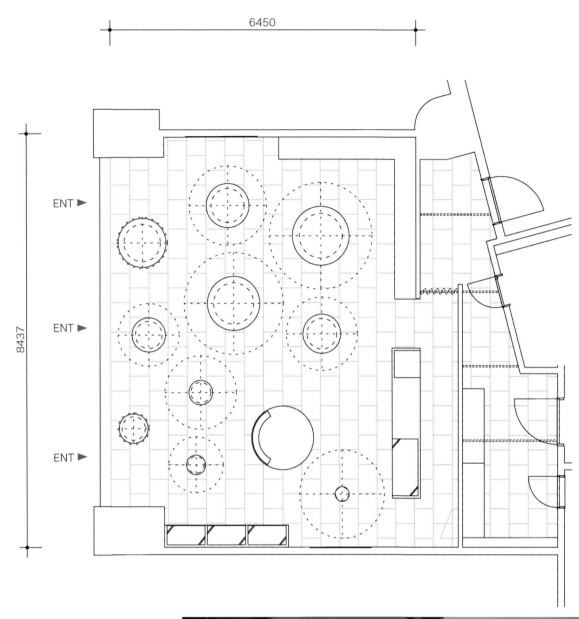

6450

8437

ENT ▶

ENT ▶

ENT ▶

Floor plan

The lighting is the most important feature in this store. Each display pedestal has its corresponding cylindrical lighting fixture that casts a clear white light over the product.

131

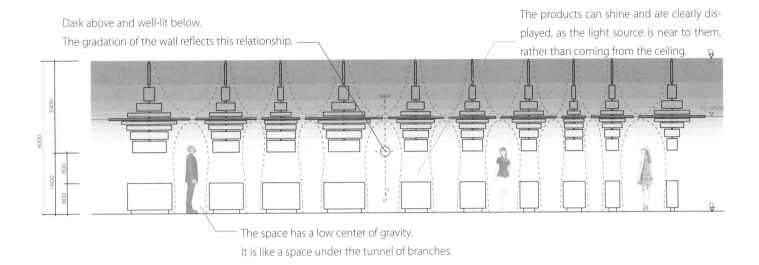

Dark above and well-lit below.
The gradation of the wall reflects this relationship.

The products can shine and are clearly displayed, as the light source is near to them, rather than coming from the ceiling.

The space has a low center of gravity.
It is like a space under the tunnel of branches.

AB Rogers Design

Emperor Moth

London, United Kingdom

Photographs: Morley Von Sternberg

Emperor Moth is a new, fresh and dynamic Russian fashion label designed by Russian fashion designer Katia Gomiashvili. Katia commissioned ARD to create a new store in Mayfair, including all the branding and packaging, which would reflect the innovative spirit of the designer. Inspired by Nikki de Saint Phalle's Tarot Garden and Robert Smithson's mirrors, the team of architects created a voluptuous internal space. Mirrors have always been a source of fascination, and their influence can be seen in many different forms of art from the Russian constructivism to the Faberge eggs. Mirrors show preciousness, dynamism, modernity and nostalgia. They are central to the concept of the new Emperor Moth store. The mirrors cover every square meter of wall and ceiling space, resulting in an ever-changing scene, where perceptions of the space depend entirely on where the shopper is standing. It becomes hard to define the boundaries of the shop and customers have to "search" for the clothes because the walls and ceiling appear to be covered in them. The explosive and dynamic designs of the product become the main decorative element; the wallpaper, the graphics, the skin, which surrounds the space. The only surface in the shop that does not change and has no mirror is the blue resin floor, which serves to help visitors orientate themselves. The floor is inspired by the sky, by the sea, by the air. It fuels the mirrors, providing a pool of color, a backdrop against which to enjoy and understand the environment. Puppetry has also been inspirational in the design of this interior. A collection of dancing puppets showcase accessories and everything that is for sale, breathing life into the space. Each of the figures is lit by a free standing high quality floodlight. This is a striking, inspirational and experiential store that showcases the wonders of Emperor Moth. Shopping in the Emperor Moth is unlike shopping anywhere else in the world. Entering this space is like entering a new environment, experiencing a new undiscovered emotion, a new type of light, a new type of space. No one who enters this space will ever forget it.

Architecture:
Ab Rogers Design

Collaborators:
D. A. Studio and Dominic Robson

Joinery:
Harry Van Rooij

Sketches:
Ab Rogers Design

propeller z

GIL fashion area 1

Vienna, Austria

Photographs: Margherita Spiluttini

A fully glazed façade opens this two-story shop onto a bustling street which itself often resembles an urban catwalk; thus the threshold between the realms of street and shop are reduced to a minimum that one does not often find.

Inside, a delicate staircase leads to the ample sales areas on the upper floor. Here, in the two spaces flanking the bridge, the gray linoleum floors merge gradually into the walls, continuing upward and folding over to form the ceiling. This shell provides a subdued background for the garments on display.

The two main spaces are connected via corridors whose walls have been expanded through the insertion of recesses formed from high-gloss, prefabricated polyester units. These recesses can be used for displaying products. At the ends of the corridors are the changing rooms, which are also constructed of industrial prefab polyester units.

The furnishings were designed especially for the GIL store, and their combination of surfaces for displaying, stacking and sitting sets a bold new precedent for retail spaces. The industrial materials and surfaces engage in a dialogue of extreme contrasts with the textures of the clothing.

With additional features like a bar, a high-end sound system (including an assortment of CDs, which are also for sale), and a projection surface, the GIL store shows how fashion has melded with other areas of contemporary culture.

Architecture:
propeller z

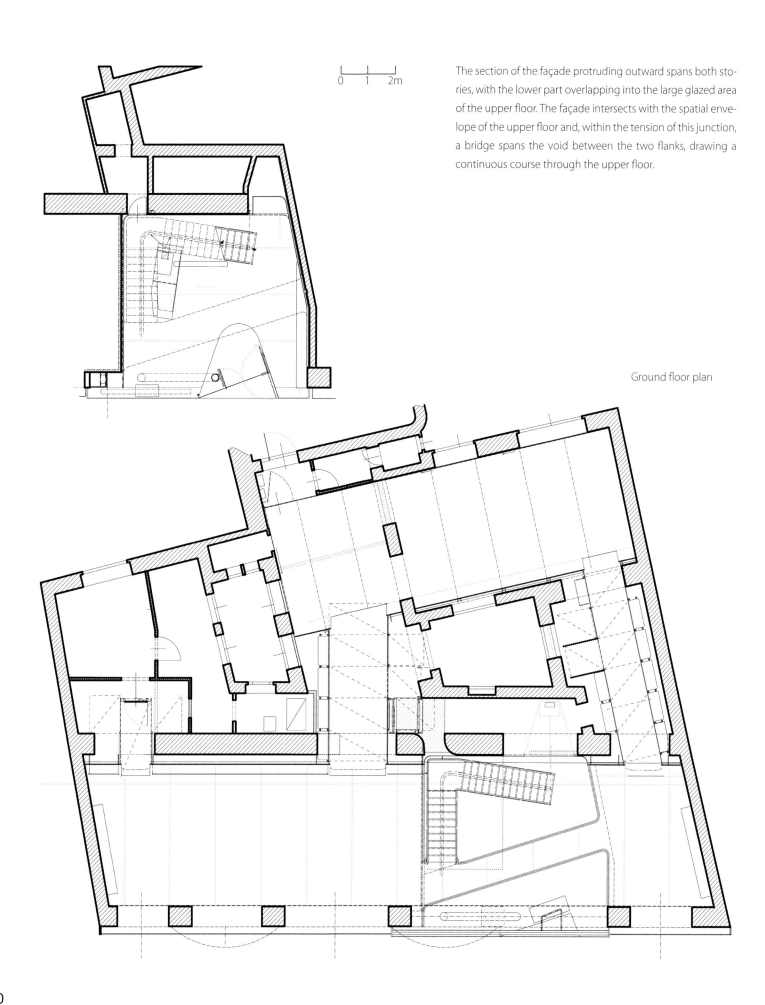

The section of the façade protruding outward spans both stories, with the lower part overlapping into the large glazed area of the upper floor. The façade intersects with the spatial envelope of the upper floor and, within the tension of this junction, a bridge spans the void between the two flanks, drawing a continuous course through the upper floor.

0   1   2m

Ground floor plan

150

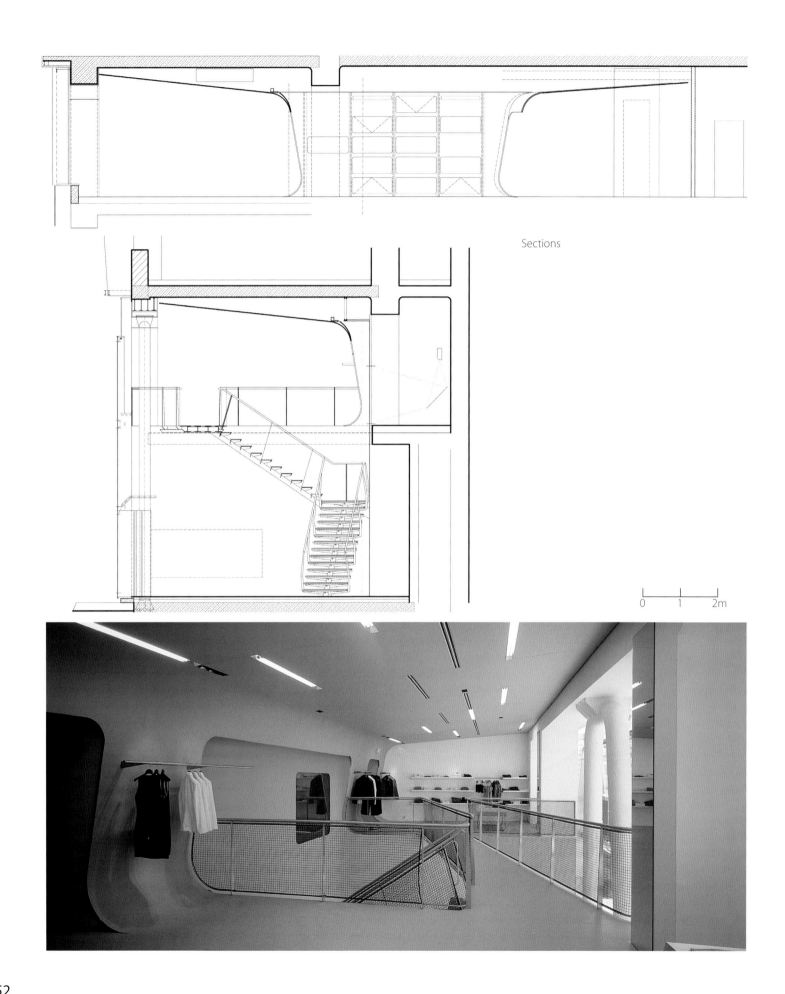

Sections

0   1   2m

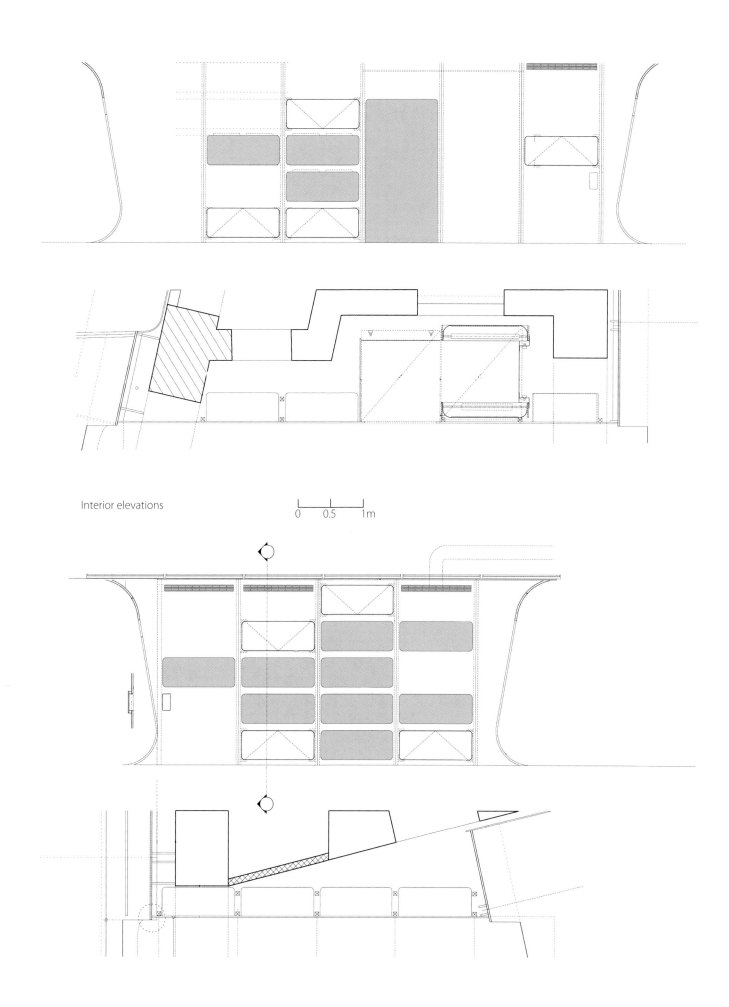

Interior elevations

0   0.5   1m

155

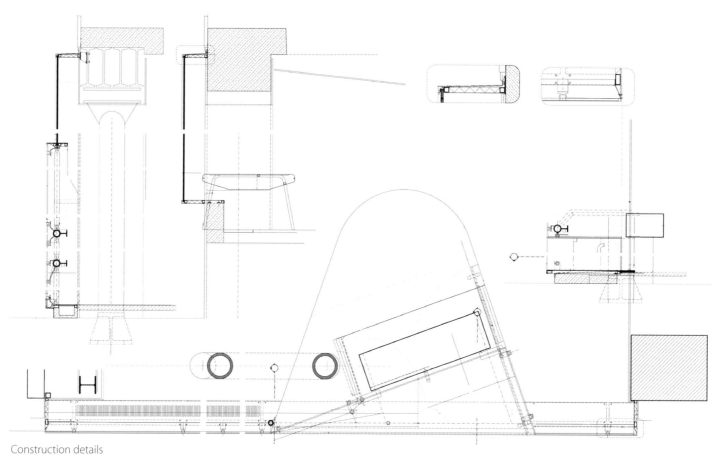

Construction details

Carbondale, Eric Carlson + Nagaishi Architects

Louis Vuitton

Nagoya, France

Photographs: Jimmy Cohrssen

The design of the Louis Vuitton, Midland Square store in Nagoya Japan is result of the collaboration of two Architects: Nagaishi Takayoshi for the façade and Eric Carlson of CARBONDALE Architects for the 600 sqm (6,500 sqft) interior. The conceptual approach for Eric Carlson was to unify the expression of the interior with that of the exterior facade to assure a singular architecture and LV brand image. Because the façade appears as a precious "gift-wrapping" enveloping the building outside, the first idea is to create inside the store a special architectural "gift" in the form of a distinctive sculpture that visitors discover upon entering. This is achieved by demolishing the floors slabs to express the 11meter high volume, then suspending a cylindrical mezzanine in the center of the void. The mezzanine itself is composed of six thousand extruded aluminum flowers capped in polished brass and stainless steel that appear to rain down from a luminous floating cloud. The interior of the cloud is lined in a warm anigrey wood and contains the largest display area of leathergoods, textiles and sunglasses.

The second idea is the transformation of the pragmatic stairs for vertical circulations into a travel experience. Inspired by the twisting metal flat bars which compose the façade, Eric superimposes two large spiral stairs, that twist around each other in a unique DOUBLE HELIX geometry. The stairs magically never meet and are reminiscent of an M.C. Escher drawing. Together the intertwining stairs look like a monument DNA molecule as they penetrate the "cloud mezzanine", connecting the 3 retail levels and uniting the Louis Vuitton brand image.

Architecture:
Carbondale, Eric Carlson +
Nagaishi Architects

Façade Design:
Nagaishi Architects, Tokyo. Nagaishi Takayoshi

Principal in charge
Samura Yoshikazu

Project Team
Architects - Interior Design:
CARBONDALE- Architects, Paris
Eric Carlson

Principal
Pierre Tortrat, Cristiano Benzoni
Associates Pierre Marescaux, Pauline Callais,
Geraldine Ecault, Celine Helfer

Project team
Associate Architects:
Higo & Associates, Tokyo

Lighting Consultant:
George Sexton Associates, Washington D.C.

General Contractor / Engineer:
Takenaka Nagoya

Interior Contractor:
Takashimaya Space Create, Tokyo

Furniture Fabrication:
East Joint, Hong Kong

Lighting Fabrication:
Yamagiwa Corporation, Tokyo

Total Area:
800 sqm (8,100 sqft)

Retail Area:
600 sqm (6,500 sqft)

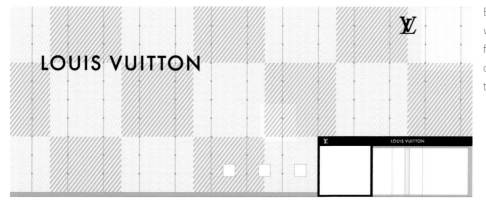

Because the façade appears as a precious "gift-wrapping" enveloping the building outside, the first idea is to create inside the store a special architectural "gift" in the form of a distinctive sculpture that visitors discover upon entering.

The mezzanine itself is composed of six thousand extruded aluminum flowers capped in polished brass and stainless steel that appear to rain down from a luminous floating cloud.

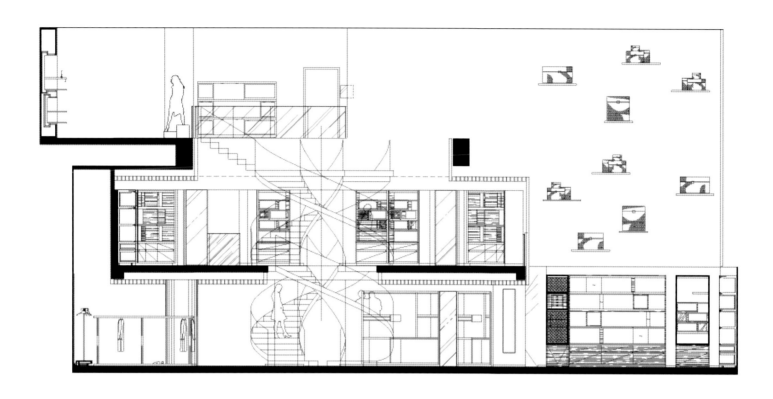

163

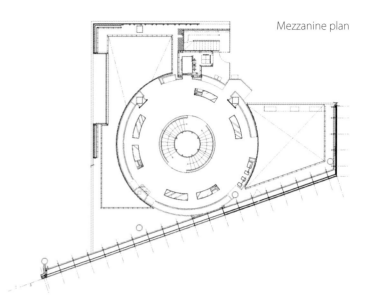

Mezzanine plan

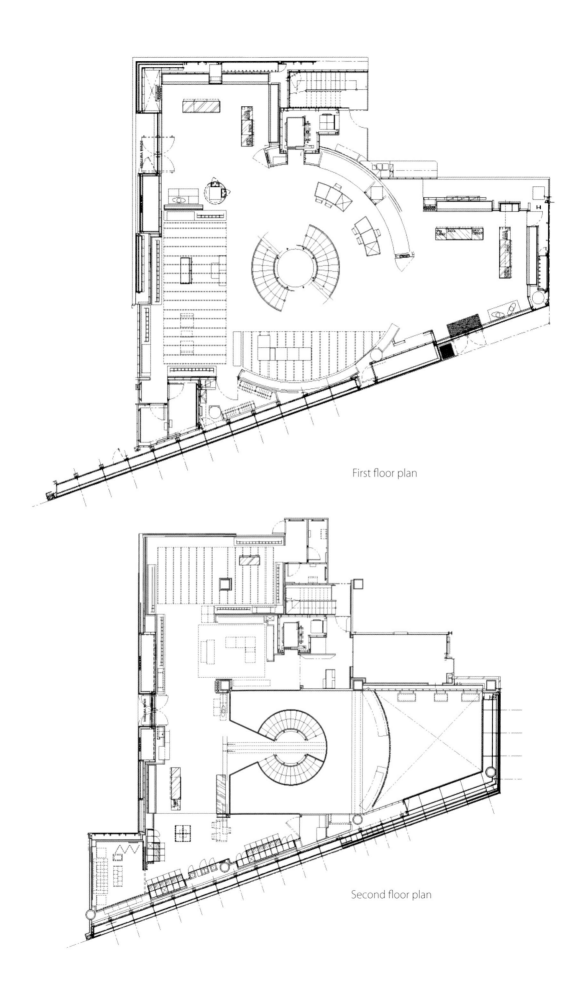

First floor plan

Second floor plan

Giorgio Borruso Design

Fornarina / Rome

Rome, Italy

Photographs: Benny Chan / FOTOWORKS

This project represents the third stage of the collaboration of Giorgio Borruso Design with Fornarina, the Italian retailer of women's fashion, shoes and accessories. In this partnership, they collaborated to recreate the Fornarina dream world in a tight 55 sqm (590 sqft) space. They had to redress the existing space within a historical building, further obstructed by a large central structural column and a gap for the staircase to the lower level storage, located very close to the front of the space. A continuous glossy surface from floor-to-walls-to-ceiling encapsulates the space in a sleek whiteness. A wall to wall mirror along one side multiplies the width.

After observing the flow of customers in other Fornarina projects, it was decided to indicate the direction of flow, to guide the customers through the interior, using the shape fo the ceiling to guide them and softening the corners of the walls to create a space that gently encourages visitors along the optimum path.

This story is about the gravitational experience around the black central element that goes through the ceiling and melts into the floor. It is a sort of tree that contains continuous surprises with every turn around it. It is like a conglomerate, a grouping of various particles, some apparently still in an embryonic state. A single observes movement around this structure. Stainless steel knobs that are interchangeable with hanging bars and ovoid shelves surround the structure and reappear around the walls. A slice of wall in mirror, pierced with chrome rings extends from the tree towards the entrance, displaying precious objects, while emphasizing the pathway around the space.

Silvery tendrils of light are frozen in motion as they are caught in the direction of the flow around the tree. The cash wrap desk in high gloss white is mirrored by a matching display that encircles the staircase spiraling down to the storage room in rhodamine red.

This work is substantially different from the two previous Fornarina collaborations at Via dei Condotti and Las Vegas, begging the question as to whether this project could be considered the chronological conclusion of past research. It the Via Cola di Rienzo project the point of arrival or of departure?

Architecture:
Giorgio Borruso Design

Openings pierce the wooden ceiling to show the internal organs, exposing HVAC ductwork, electrical conduits, pipes, and cables, all in Rhodamine Red, Fornarina's signature color.

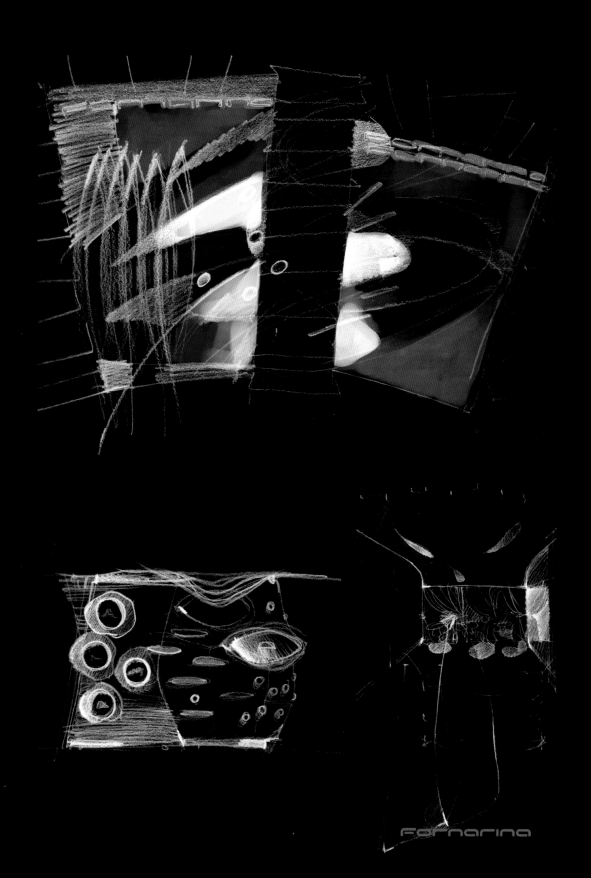

Fornarina

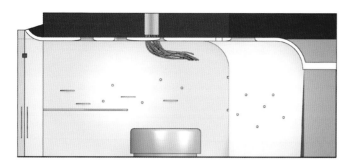

Section AA

Section EE

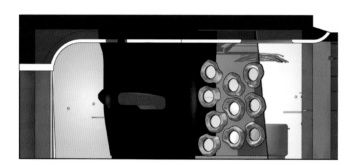

Section BB

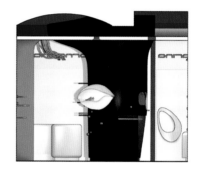

Section FF

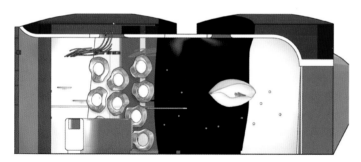

Section CC

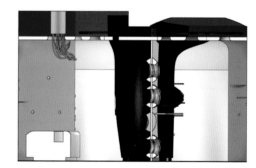

Section GG

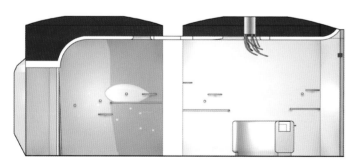

Section DD

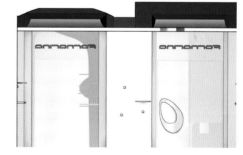

Section EE

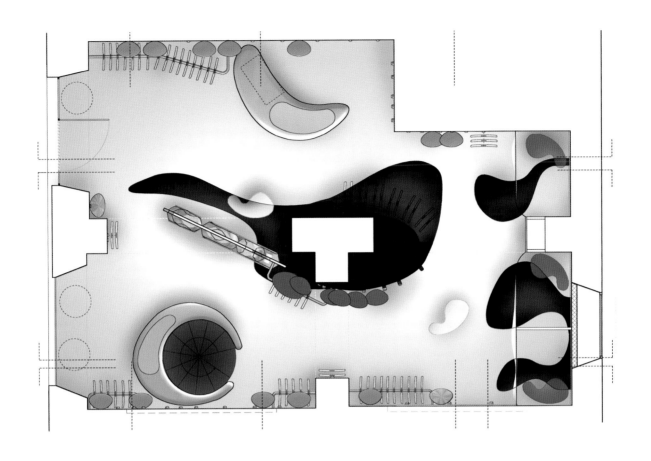

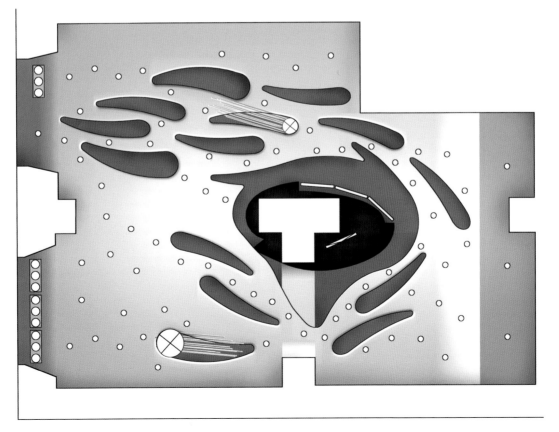

177

Across the back, a white velvet curtain wall masks the dressing rooms, while tongues of black resin flooring reach out from beneath, teasing the viewer with what may be behind.

Asymptote Architecture

Carlos Miele Flagship Store

New York, USA   **Photographs:** Paul Warchol, courtesy of Carlos Miele

Asymptote's design for the new Manhattan flagship for fashion designer Carlos Miele celebrates Miele's unique perspective and aesthetic attitude toward design in his native country, Brazil. The design and architecture of the store embraces a culture that champions modern aesthetics while being steeped in traditional cultural rituals and aesthetics. These aspects found in Miele's own work were the inspiration for the environment which is at once a hybrid of both a shopping environment as it is a sophisticated and sculpted backdrop on which to display. The overall atmosphere of the space is shaped as much by the exuberant vivacity of Brazilian culture as it is by the coolness and precision afforded by new technological means of fabrication, reflected in both the clothes and architectural elements. This contemporary setting of seemingly disparate but not irreconcilable opposites influences and sets the stage for the presentation of Miele's oeuvre, creating a compelling spatial and visual experience. Asymptote's design for the Carlos Miele Flagship was decidedly conceived of as a bright open space utilizing a neutral palette of white and shades of pale green/ green blue and gray all serving to foreground Miele's colorful clothing design. The interior space consists of two tone high gloss epoxy flooring with imbedded neon and halogen lighting set beneath tempered glass rings. The curved formed steel hanging displays that are cantilevered from the walls sit above lacquered bent plywood display units below. At the storefront window display areas as well as the circular change-room environment are backlit illuminated floor and walls using 3M diffusion film, plexiglas and fluorescent lighting. The ceiling which is a contoured surface is formed from a high-gloss stretched pvc based material produced by Barrisol. For both the design and fabrication of the curved forms and surfaces in the store computer generated drawings and digital procedures were instrumental. Additionally, there are two 'Asymptote' video installations featuring digital art have been integrated into the architecture of the store. Each piece celebrating an aspect of body and spatiality. These works are extensions of Asymptote's art projects recently included in Documenta XI and the Venice Biennale.

Architecture:
Asymptote Architecture

Section & Plan

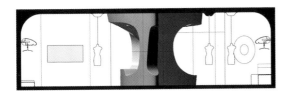

The centerpiece of the store is a large floor to ceiling sculptural form that traverses the entire length of the interior space. This 'alter' element is used for both seating and display and is fabricated from lacquer finished bent plywood over a rib and gusset sub-structure that was laser cut directly from CAD drawings and fabricated off site.

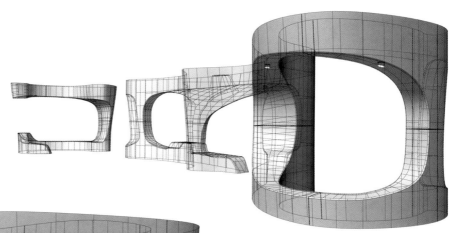

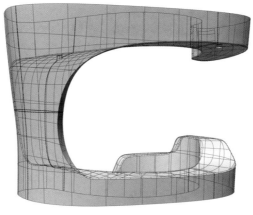

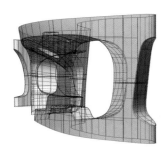

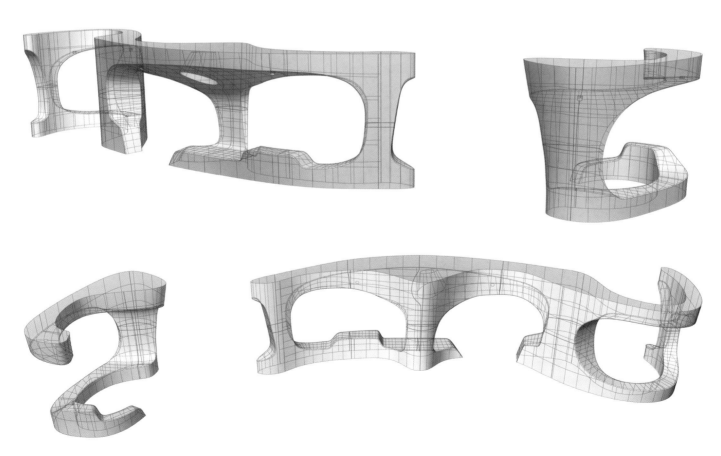

The architecture is a 'place' for gathering, meandering and viewing all thought of as as rituals which are set against a landscape that celebrates desire and the sensual.

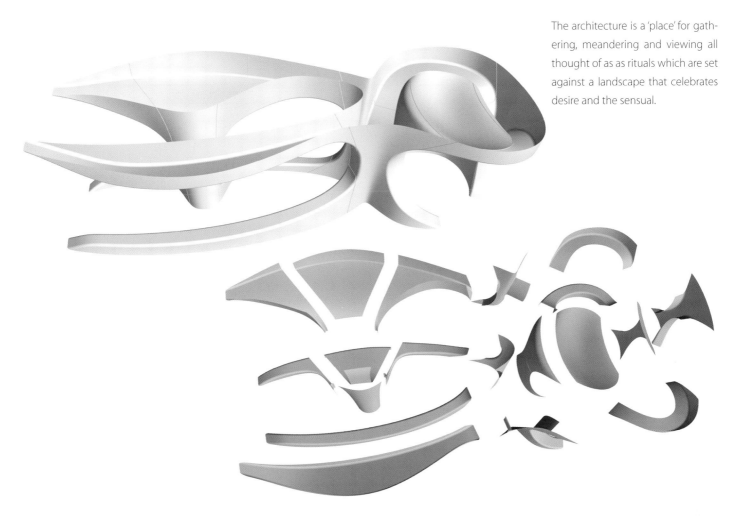

Heatherwick Studio

La Maison Unique

New York, USA Photographs: Nic Lehoux

Longchamp's new flagship store, La Maison Unique, located in downtown SoHo, New York is this prestigious fashion company's one hundredth boutique worldwide, as well as its new professional trade showroom. Its spectacularly big floor shop surface area occupies over 830 sqm (9000 sqft) and offers the brand's full line of women's and men's fashion accessories. The sheer volume of this 1936 building, its wide-open, single room spaciousness with high ceilings and unique structural details immediately struck the Cassegrain family, who have run the French luxury brand, Longchamp since its inception in 1948. Ideally located in the heart of SoHo on the corner of Spring and Greene Streets, the space is So-Ho's only two-story building. The unusual characteristic of this store is that most of the space is on the second floor. The design therefore had to play on the customers' expectations with an artistic solution that enticed people up to the main retail level. Longchamp entrusted its interior design to the creative eye of London designer Thomas Heatherwick. The volume of the space is brilliantly and innovatively characterized with touches of humor here and there and is in perfect harmony with the key brand values of Longchamp: chic, creativity, pleasure, appealingly fresh. As stated by Philippe Cassegrain, CEO of Longchamp, "This project is in no way a new sales concept to be deployed the world over, It is, however, a unique architectural ensemble to be appreciated as a one-of-a-kind event." Heatherwick is known for his unconventional lines, shapes and engineering challenges and his designs are often perceived to be more sculptural than architectural. One of the most remarkable features of this store are the ribbon like forms that decorate the spaces between the staircases. These create a magic carpet effect that beckons shoppers up to the second floor. Natural light from the glazed core, which has been cut into the building, also helps to draw people up to the next level. The shopping space boasts innovative display systems, among which are shelving units, used to display part of the brand's handbag collection, which seem to have been peeled down from the ceiling. The boutique's exceptional corner location allows for the perimeter of the building to be lined with tall and wide windows which capture a plethora of natural light that in turn spreads throughout the entire space. The project also includes the construction of a third floor that houses the Longchamp showroom and an office area, and features a garden terrace.

Architecture:
Heatherwick Studio

Contractor:
Shawmut Design and Construction

Architect:
Atmosphere Design Group LLC

Expediter:
Outsource Consultants Inc

Structural Engineer:
Building Structural Engineering Services &
Gilsanz
Murray Steficek LLP

MEP Consultant:
O'Dea Lynch Abbattista & Associates

Lighting Designer:
HDLC Architectural Lighting Design

Balustrade Panels:
Talbot Designs Ltd

Metal Work:
Hillside Ironworks

Wood Work:
Imperial Woodworking Enterprises, Inc

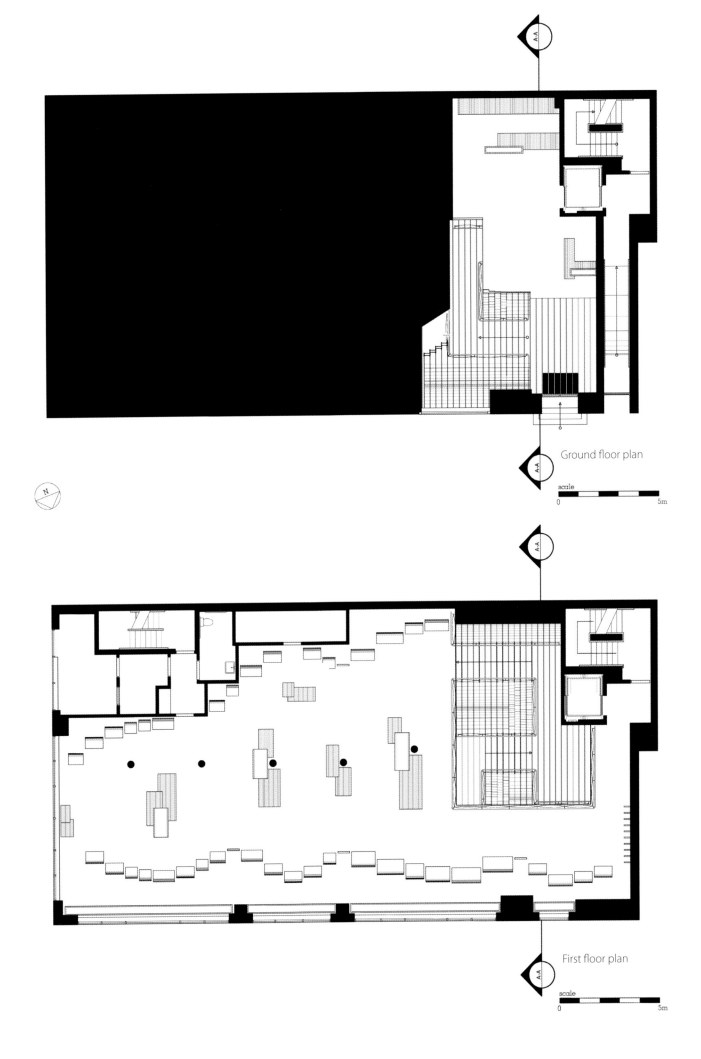

N

Ground floor plan

scale
0 ——————— 5m

First floor plan

scale
0 ——————— 5m

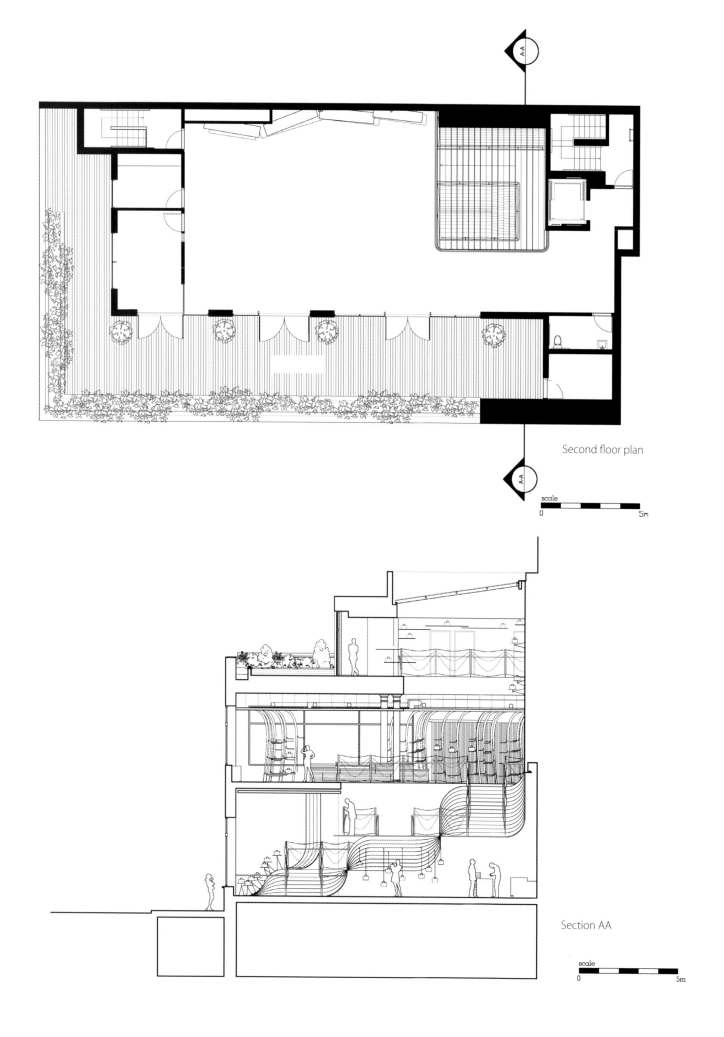

Second floor plan

scale
0 _____ 5m

Section AA

scale
0 _____ 5m

195

197

The shopping space boasts innovative display systems, among which are shelving units, used to display part of the brand's handbag collection, which seem to have been peeled down from the ceiling. The boutique's exceptional corner location allows for the perimeter of the building to be lined with tall and wide windows which capture a plethora of natural light that in turn spreads throughout the entire space.

Patrick Jouin

Boutique Van Cleef & Arpels

Paris, France

Photographs: Eric Laingel

Architecture:
Patrick Jouin
Project team:
Laurent Janvier, Karri Campbell

With 58 boutiques throughout the world, Van Cleef & Arpels wanted to honor their centennial year by celebrating their Parisian origins at Place Vendôme, a symbol of French good taste. Designed by Mansart in the early eighteenth century, the Place Vendôme features arcades along the ground floor and two upper floors of wide windows between pairs of pilasters under pediments. Set into the roof are "bull's eye" and dormer windows. John Law, regarded as the father of the modern stock exchange, acquired more than half of the buildings around the square in 1718, drawing other prominent citizens in his wake. During the Napoleonic period, the square was chosen by Napoleon to erect a monumental column cast from the melted-down iron of 1,250 canons captured at the Battle of Austerlitz in 1805. Demolished during the "Paris Commune", the painter Courbet was bankrupted when forced to pay for its reconstruction. This column features in the Van Cleef & Arpels logo and in some of their creations The boutique's location has always been associated with quality and style, and when Alfred Van Cleef, Estelle Arpels and her brother Charles opened the original salon here in 1906, the destiny of Van Cleef & Arpels was set. Totally redistributing the 1732 sq.ft site, young designer Patrick Jouin has combined audacious fantasy and natural motifs with the classic architecture of Place Vendôme in a manner typical of this clients' philosophy, an even more perfect frame for their latest creations.

Order and purity interact with contemporary curves throughout the boutique, forming a long, smooth arabesque on the back wall. Growing out of the arabesque is a garland of Art Deco roses surrounded by leaves fairies, butterflies and dragonflies. Created by a skilled master plasterer after drawings by Patrick Jouin, each rosebud was gilded with pure white gold, lending the entire space a feeling of luxury and springtime freshness. Four master cabinetmakers worked as a team to carve the varying pattern of leaves, flowers, butterflies and dragonflies onto the oak paneling. Each panel was treated to remove tannins, lightened, stained and finally polished to obtain a subtle luster. Special lighting brings out this sublime creation in wood.

A stunning chandelier of innumerable Murano glass spheres hangs in the circular atrium between the two floors and oval mirrors mounted on the ceiling at different angles reflect the light through the room. The wool carpet goes from a light sand color at the door to deep brown at the back. Two immense display cabinets emerge like islands of color among the beiges and browns. Jewelry is also displayed in circular cases set in the columns, to be seen from all sides. Patrick Jouin has designed chairs and display desks that are welcoming yet neutral enough to set off the jewelry. Hervé Descottes has created small adjustable table lamps, so staff members can "spotlight" a piece of jewelry for the visitor to see while preserving the confidentiality of the meeting.

The original salons have been dedicated to illustrate Van Cleef & Arpels' creativity, showing a collection of their historic designs, photographs of the celebrities who have worn them and stills from films in which their shop and their jewelry appeared.

Order and purity interact with contemporary curves throughout the boutique, forming a long, smooth arabesque on the back wall. Growing out of the arabesque is a garland of Art Deco roses surrounded by leaves, fairies, butterflies and dragonflies.

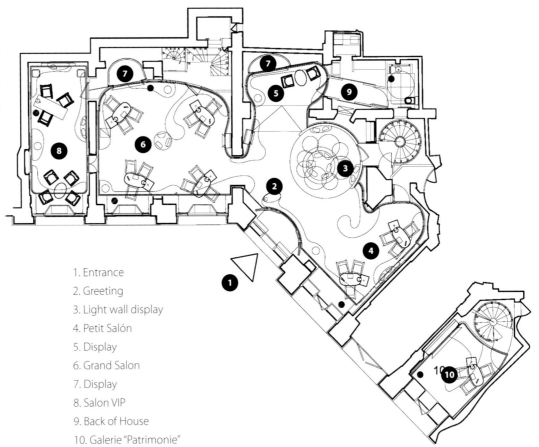

1. Entrance
2. Greeting
3. Light wall display
4. Petit Salón
5. Display
6. Grand Salon
7. Display
8. Salon VIP
9. Back of House
10. Galerie "Patrimonie"

ADD+ (Manuel Bailo, Rosa Rull)

Sita Murt Boutique (Avinyó Street)

Barcelona, Spain

Photographs: Giovanni Zanzi

The project for the shop Sita Murt began when, during an initial visit to the site (a small, ground floor space), a stairway leading to a basement with a barrel vault ceiling was discovered. The wish to incorporate this space into the overall design scheme led to the idea of punching openings into the vaulted ceiling to bring air and light into the basement's darkest recesses.

From the start, the construction process was presented as an exercise in metal. First was the pick-up drill work and the creation of a number of holes in varying diameters done with an orderly repetition of precise, 20-centimeter socket punches, the end result being a series of flowery buttonholes. Next came the placing of structural light fittings made of curved sheet metal. Via their anchorage system to the vault of the ceiling, the light fixtures help redistribute the load that these very same openings had destabilized. Finally, a network of curved and bent metal tubes was suspended from the ceilings, weaving their way throughout the space, turning the light openings into buttonholes.

Given its concentrated structural capacity, construction in metal enables both a reduction in width and thickness of the elements used and an increase in their amount of available length for support.

The anchorage for the eight-millimeter curved sheet metal structural caps supports the ceramic vault covering the basement, thus enabling their perforation. Being higher than is strictly necessary, these structural sheet metal elements also serve as lighting fixtures and display cases.

The two sections of curved and bent metal tubes (of three and ten centimeters in diameter) which sew the space together from top to bottom with the minimum number of auxiliary pieces, serve to support the stairway as well as provide hangers on which clothes can be displayed.

The dimensions of both the ground floor and the basement, and the way they have been treated as two different containers, suggested the use of a single color in each space. The design scheme thereby plays up the contrast created between the two levels through the interplay of openings.

Architecture:
ADD+ (Manuel Bailo, Rosa Rull)

For the choice of color on the ground floor and façade, a preliminary study of the range of colors seen in the new shops which have sprung up recently on Calle Avinyó (viewed as a representative sample of those that have opened throughout Barcelona's old city) was conducted. Among the spectrum of bright colors available, that corresponding to the address of number 18 was chosen.

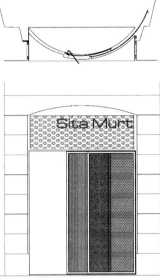

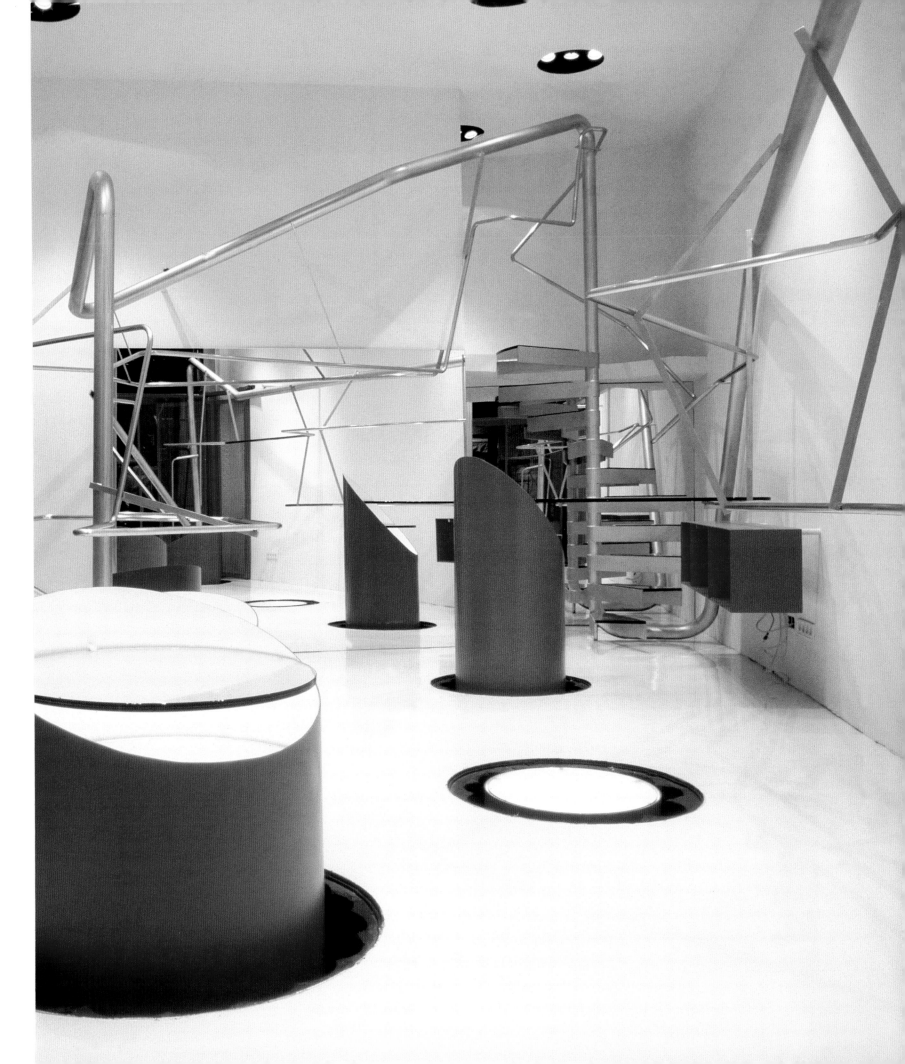

Detail of one of the skylights

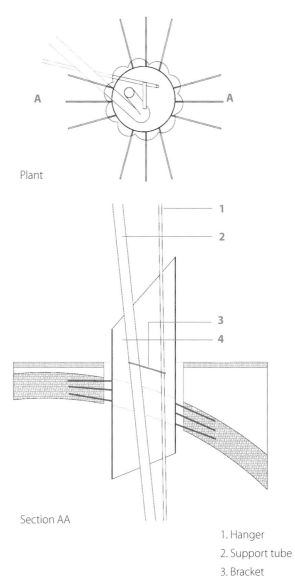

Plant

Section AA

1. Hanger
2. Support tube
3. Bracket
4. Vault

Unfolding of the vault retaining sheet

upper floor level

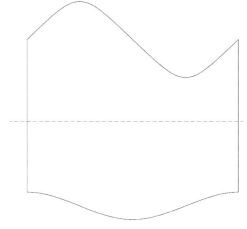

223

Asymptote:
Hani Rashid, Lise Anne Couture

Alessi Flagship Store

130 Greene Street, New York, USA

Photographs: Elizabeth Felicelia

Alessi, a world-recognized brand helped set the pace for design objects in the 1980's with the production of iconic works from critical postmodern architects ranging from Aldo Rossi to Michael Graves. In subsequent years, a highly unique and respected image for the company evolved from the creativity and insight of Alessandro Mendini and his strong relationship with Alberto Alessi. In a deliberate and significant turn in the road, Alberto Alessi personally engaged Hani Rashid and Asymptote to develop an entirely new trajectory for the Alessi brand. The company engaged Asymptote in not only new product design, but also in creating a new graphic identity for the brand and in creating the new flagship store opening in the heart of Soho in New York City.

Asymptote's approach to the store, product and brand design developed from a search for new languages predicated on mathematically inspired and derived elegance. In a radical shift away from the postmodern staples of historic pastiche, motif, vivid coloration, and iconographic and symbolic form, Asymptote forged an approach that took its cues from fluid and dynamic movement. This approach, intrinsic in new methods and instigated by digital tools and means, privileges a tectonic play of sophisticated geometric solutions in place of symbolic gestures.

The strategic shift in the aesthetic and formal approach that Asymptote has adopted is not only tied intrinsically to the body of work the studio has pursued over the years (melding digital potentials with actualized spatial, programmatic and formal outcomes) but is also a means by which to navigate the new generations of architects and designers now engaged in Alessi design initiatives. Like Asymptote, many of these designers (Massimilano Fuksas, Weil Arets, Greg Lynn, and Toyo Ito, among others) are all in search of new and intriguing languages that steer clear of the emblematic aspects residual from post-modernity.

Architecture:
Asymptote

Client:
Alessi US Shops

Principal Architects:
Hani Rashid +
Lise Anne Couture

Project Architect:
Jill Leckner

Design Team:
Stella Lee, David Lessard, Carsten Laursen,
Karen Lee, Jong Kouk Kim, Erick Carcamo,
Asako Hiraoka-Sperry

Assistants:
Jenny Chow, Ruben Useche, Salvador Lopez,
Natalia Ibañez Lario, Carlo Kessler,
Marcia Akermann

Structural Engineer:
Robert Silman Associates
Nat Oppenheimer, Partner

MEP Engineer:
Kam Chiu Associates

Lighting Consultant:
Tillotson Design Associates Suzan Tillotson,
Partner

Contractor:
Fountainhead Construction

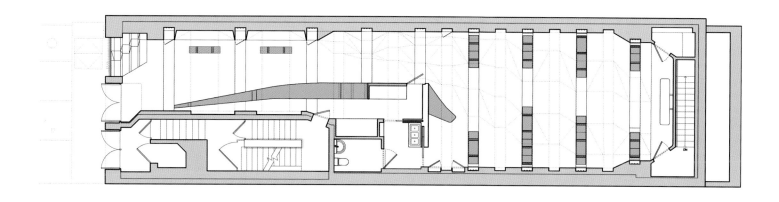

Northwest section

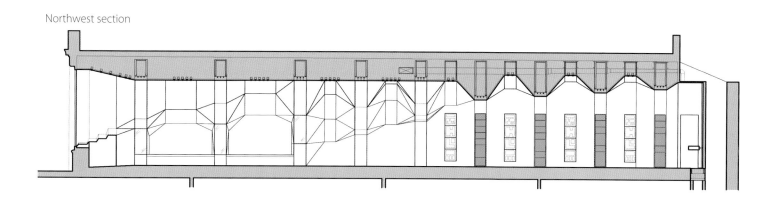

Southest section

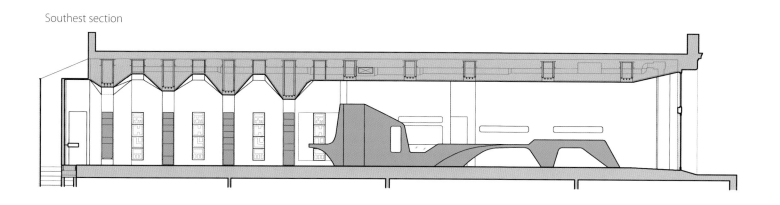

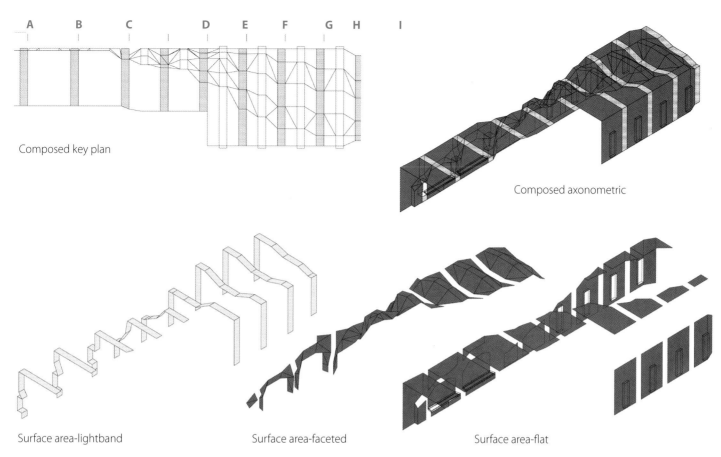

Composed key plan

Composed axonometric

Surface area-lightband

Surface area-faceted

Surface area-flat

229

Sean Dix

Byblos Boutique

Moscow, Russia

Photographs: Ramak Fazel

The Italian clothing line Byblos commissioned Sean Dix to create its new retail image for their boutique in Moscow, which showcases the women's, men's, and accessories collections. Ribbons of light, syncopated geometric volumes, elaborately textured surfaces, glowing elements and structure as design are all the elements which the designer has brought together to form this new retail concept. This new Byblos space is defined by continuous and decisive changes in rhythm: precise lines bending into curves then shifting rapidly to angles, encounters between reflective and opaque surfaces, the play of light and textured shadow.The inspiration for the project came from two main premises: the first, the designer's respect for the Byblos logo, its play of angles and curves, straight lines and arcs. The designer's intention was for the project to recall that same kind of contrasting harmony present in the logo and to define the space with architecture. This, according to Dix, was to be the "signature of Byblos."The interior is framed by a decisive rigorous geometry- a defining architecture of alternately rising and falling beams and tapering columns- which delimits this complex environment. The textured walls are in movement- a surface of three-dimensional waves- created using a special technique, which incises geometric patterns into composite ones in a computerized bas-relief. The display cases virtually float: each flaring out in a dramatic arc, balanced on a miniscule base. Again they propose the encounter between straight and curved lines, the contrast between curves and sharp edges. Their finish is a special rubber coating, a rich, light-absorbing surface that begs to be touched. The display tables designed for the space are composed of an infinity of thin swooping steel ribbons. Though the form is defined, there is no volume, and it is possible to see through the object to what lies beyond. The garment display system, created especially for Byblos, breaks with the traditional method: the hangers have no hooks, inexplicably suspended from the rail by hidden magnets. Captured between the central columns of the main walls are glowing bands of shelves, created using special light-conducting plastics. The effect is that of rigorous simplicity. Two glowing white chandeliers, designed by Dix, are located at the entrance of the boutique. Hundreds of thin, glowing arcs define the exterior of these hollow forms, creating an optical effect like vibrating bands of light. A ribbon of light runs the entire perimeter of the space, emphasizing the geometric rhythm of the columns and beams, becoming in itself a decorative element.The colors of this project play between shifts in tone: a complex palette of grays and whites alternate, some lacquered, others opaque, some rubber, some velvet. The only true colors are used as accents- modern, almost fluorescent, dirty green and yellow.

Architecture:
Sean Dix

The garment display system, created especially for Byblos, breaks with the traditional method: the clothes hangers have no hooks, inexplicably suspended from the rail by hidden magnets.Captured between the central columns of the main walls are glowing bands of shelves, created using special light-conducting plastics

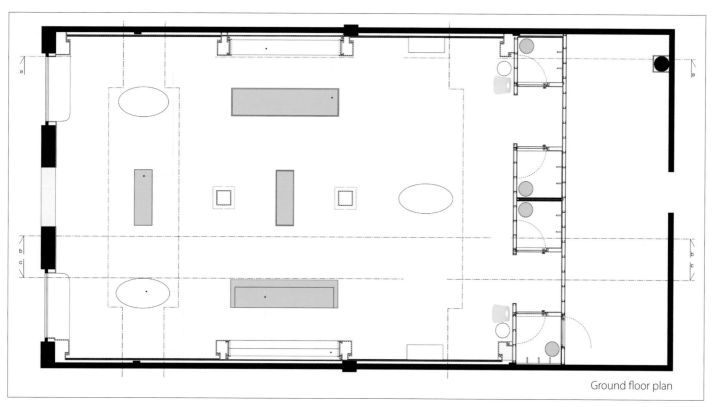

Ground floor plan

The inspiration for the project was born from two main premises: the first, the designer's respect for the Byblos logo, its play of angles and curves, straight lines and arcs.

The designer's intention was for the project to recall that same kind of contrasting harmony present in the logo and to define the space with architecture.

Randy Brown Architects

Bizarre

Omaha, Nebraska, USA   **Photographs:** Farshid Assassi

This 130 sqm (1,400 sqft) space has been designed for an upscale paper store that specializes in unique paper art objects. The owner requested a store design that would help them to organize the merchandise into groups and categories. In a bid to facilitate the process of finding solutions without being hampered by either past experiences or established expectations, the design team established a process. It was based on three main aims: to experiment with new ways to maximize the space; to create continuity between the store fixtures and the interior surfaces, and to design a delicate and fluid context akin to the paper art objects the shop would specialize in.

The interior space developed from experiments with the folding and cutting of a piece of paper, simplifying the design language. This continuous surface bends and folds to display merchandise and conceal the mechanical, electrical and structural systems. The space plan accentuates the long narrow bay by separating the store into an open space and a more enclosed space. The open space plan proposes a series of pods, constructed with clear glass and plastic, in which to organize the different sorts of merchandise. The intention is to create as much transparency as possible, so that the objects appear to float in the space. The magic comes from the lightness and transparency of the design, precisely those qualities that this installation seeks to transmit as values in their own right. The more enclosed space houses the checkout desk, restrooms and a stair leading to a mezzanine above

During the design phase, a new retail idea evolved which the team called "drop and shop." The idea is to create a secure children's play area where mom's can drop off the kids while shopping in the store. From the lower playroom, with toys and games, a flight of stairs leads to the clubhouse that overlooks the store, allowing mothers to keep an eye on their children while shopping.

Besides supplying space for all the ductwork to be concealed, the direct correspondence between the nature of the design and the nature of the merchandise present the viewer with a poetic statement, a coherent environment in which the small and delicate cohabits with the large and enveloping.

Architecture:
Randy Brown

RBA collaborators:
Randy Brown AIA

Principal in charge:
Dirk Henke, Scott Newland,
Lee Shradar, Brian Garvey,
Zach Hilleson

General contractor:
Randy Brown Architects

The interior space developed from experiments with the folding and cutting of a piece of paper, simplifying the design language. This continuous surface bends and folds to display merchandise and conceal the mechanical, electrical and structural systems.

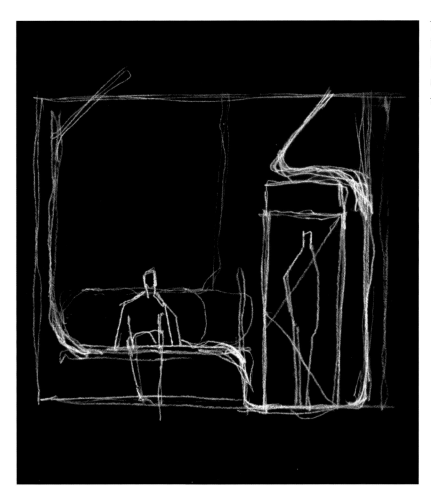

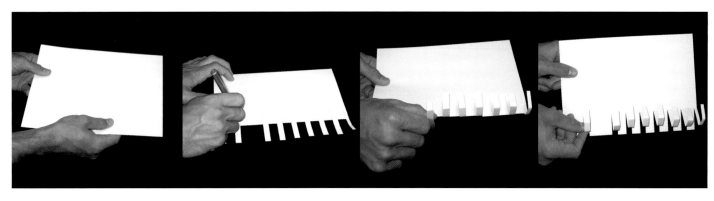

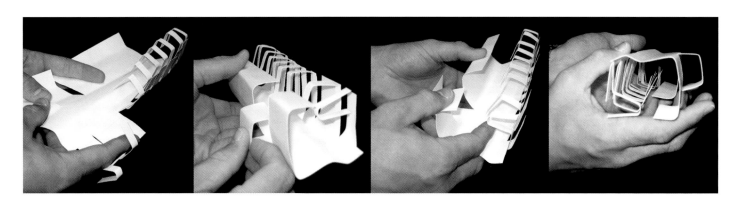

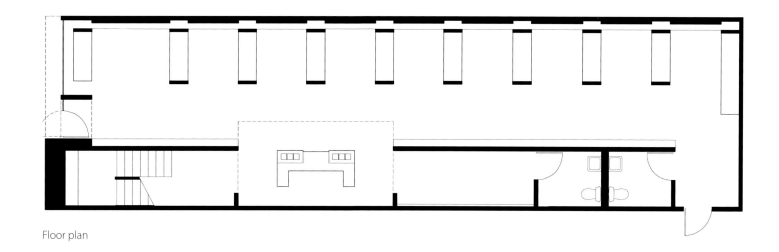

Floor plan

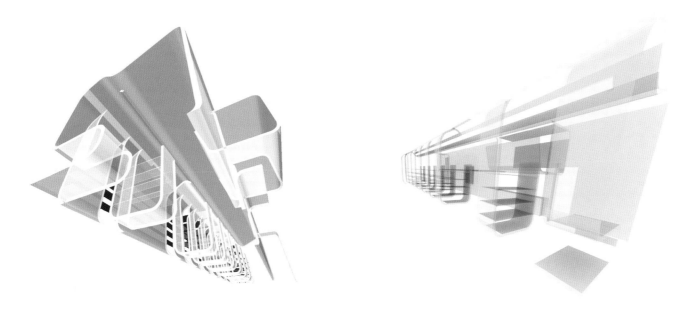

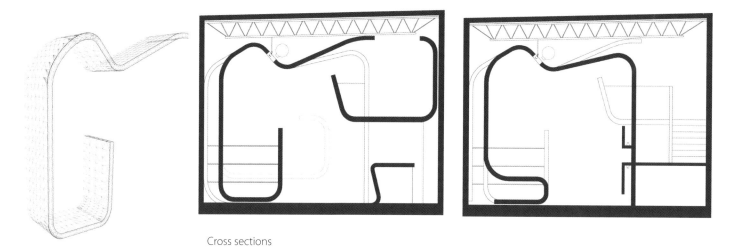

Cross sections

251

Corneille Uedingslohmann

Little Red Riding Hood GmbH

Berlin, Germany   **Photographs:** Joachim Wagner

Architecture:
Corneille Uedingslohmann

The story of Little Red Riding Hood is the world of fashion label LRRH. With its newly opened flagship store in Berlin Mitte, it offers an area for fashion, accessories, books and music within the context of the Grimm narrative. The inventory consists of: mannequins with wolf heads, clothes, shoes and jewelry. It also features beautifully illustrated books from different countries, which show the well-known fairy tale, along with magazines like 'Alert' and 'Parkett' alongside the latest CDs.

With the opening of its flagship store, LRRH gives life to a completely new sales concept, which is a symbiosis of fashion, art and modern media spread over two stories. The newest Prêt à Porter creations of the label are presented beside selected assortments of fashion, accessories, recent books, radio plays and music. The planned exhibitions which will rotate every three months will include artists from fashion, media and performance art. With every new presentation LRRH hopes to allow the artists to represent themselves from their own standpoint as well as show the connection between the performer and the label.

The spatial realization of the store was conceived as a three-dimensional scene of this fantastic fairy tale. It comprises one space divided into two levels. With a size of only 33sqm on the ground floor, the entrance is reduced to its bare function. The stairwell flows by a large projection screen that depicts the surreal images akin to the world of the fairy tale and into the basement which is ten times larger. The interior of the construction is formed from white fiberglass and is a contrast to the heterogeneous surrounding of the Friedrichstrasse and fades out the external world in favor of that of the fairy tale one in the basement.

The cross section of the wall covering is constantly changing and forms niches, curvatures and recesses for the presentation of merchandise. The production quality of the individual elements is exemplary. In Germany there are hardly any examples of this technology in a continuous form especially in this order of magnitude. Even if design and conception as well as the computer files represent an ideal basis for a file-to-factory procedure, such a process remains to be one of prototypes, compromise and persistence. The use of a 3-D plotter, as in the stereo lithography, is for this type of project somewhat unrealistic due to the fact that they can only produce small objects.

1. Friedrichstrasse
2. Exhibition
3. Sales
4. Air space
5. Projector
6. Ground floor
7. Basement

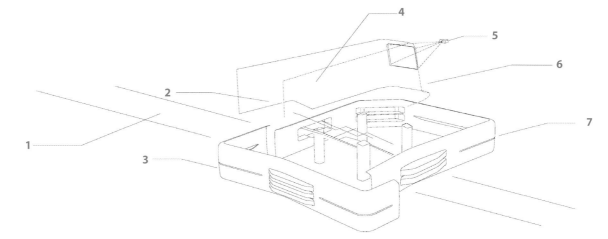

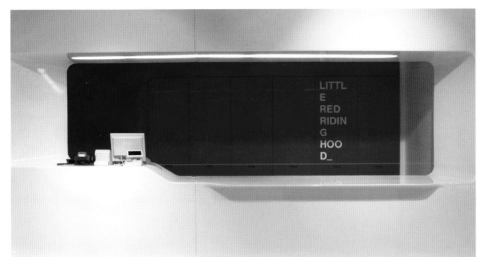

The exposed ceiling with its visible ductwork and lighting fixtures increases the dreamlike effect of the wall coverings due to their strong contrast. The flooring is also left raw with an unpolished lacquer finish and functions mainly as a backdrop for the precisely planned and constructed wall surfaces. The computer-generated 'continuous loop' fiberglass form was prefabricated into 7 meter sections and positioned on-site.

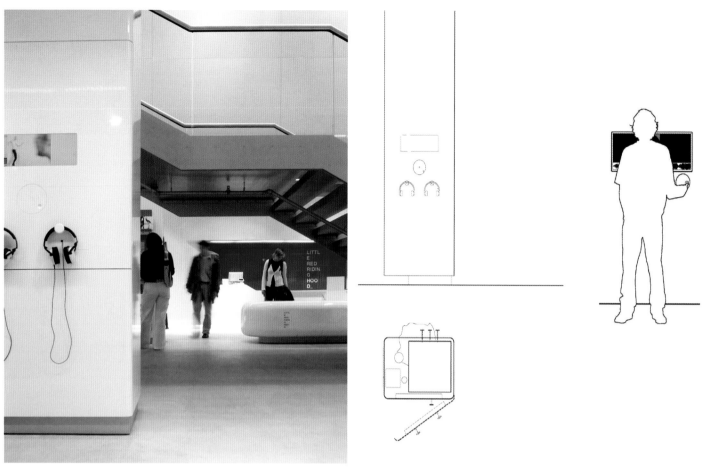

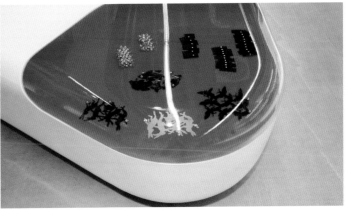

Ron Arad Associates

Y's Store

Roppongi Hills, Tokyo, Japan

Photographs: Nacása and Partners

Ron Arad Associates (RAA) were approached by Yohji Yamamoto Inc. early in 2003, to design the new store for their Prêt-a-Porter range – "Y's", to be situated within the new prestigious Roppongi Hills development in the heart of Tokyo.

The store occupies a 570 sqm (6,100 sqft) area, more or less centrally divided by 3 large structural columns. From early on in the design phase, Ron Arad Associates (RAA) decided to mask these columns in such a way as to create the illusion of lightness and movement within the space. Strong reference was drawn from the mechanical automobile parking turntables prevalent in Tokyo, and it was decided that 4 such turntables would be embedded within the floor (3 'real' columns and 1 'fake' one), to allow the main design elements within the space to pirouette gently, transforming the space constantly. In this way, the store's ceiling and floor seem to be held apart by four ever-changing sculptural elements. The store reconfigures itself during the course of an average shopping visit. At night, the speed of rotation quickens, making the transformation of the space more palpable.

Each of these rotating 'sculptures' is in fact made of 34 aluminum tubular loops, stacked to occupy the entire distance between floor and ceiling around steel column casings. Each of these loops can be rotated a full 360º, thus accommodating an infinite number of spatial arrangements. The loops are used as hanging rails for Y's clothes, and can be transformed into wide shelves using special customized 'plug-in' units.

Additional product display is facilitated through a series of angular glass-fibre-reinforced-plastic (GRP) shelves which can 'dock' into each other to form free-standing shelf stacks, or into slats in the wall behind. The till unit is formed of a topography of displaced identical angular plates, mimicking both the shelves, and the rotating loops.

The store's changing rooms form the backdrop to the loop stacks, and are sited behind gill-like curved walls which negate the need for sheltering doors or screens. Coloured LED lights signify from the outside whether a room is occupied or not.

The street-facing façade is composed of an array of curved glass panels, forming a refractory glass 'corduroy', distorting and stretching the contents of the store from the outside.

The revolving store entrance door is adorned with 4 layers of coloured glass pieces forming a freehand "Y's" logo, which when the door is spun, shimmer and change colour.

Architecture:
Ron Arad Associates

Principal Designer:
Ron Arad

Project Architect:
Asa Bruno

Team:
James Foster, Paul Gibbons

Executive Architect (Tokyo):
Studio Mebius (Shiro Nakada, Satoru Ishihara)

Principal Contractor:
Build Co. Ltd. (Japan), Minoru Kawamura

Loop Contractor:
Marzorati-Ronchetti, Italy (Roberto Travaglia)

Floor Contractor:
ABC Flooring, Japan

Lighting Consultant:
iGuzzini, Italy

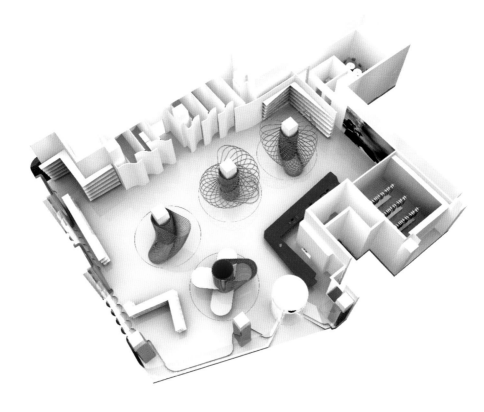

General arrangement plan

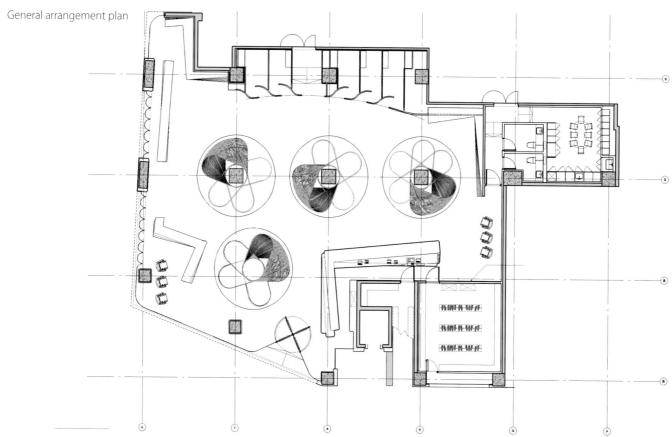

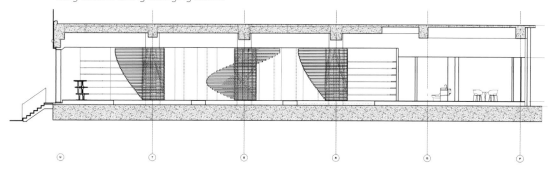

Long section facing changing rooms

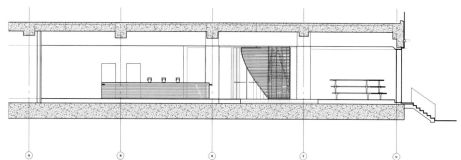

Long section facing counter

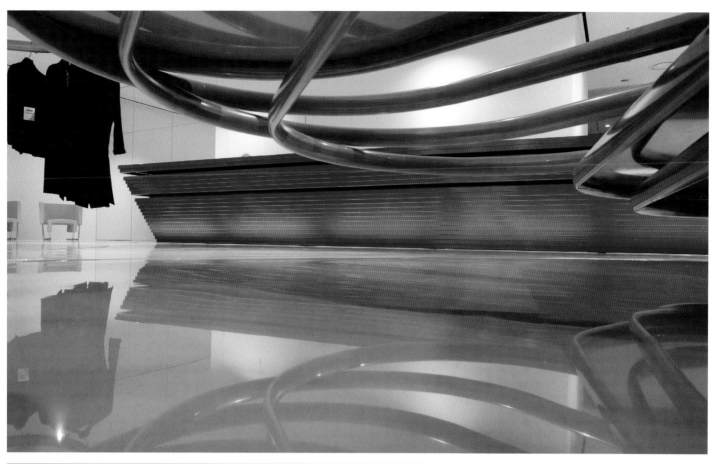

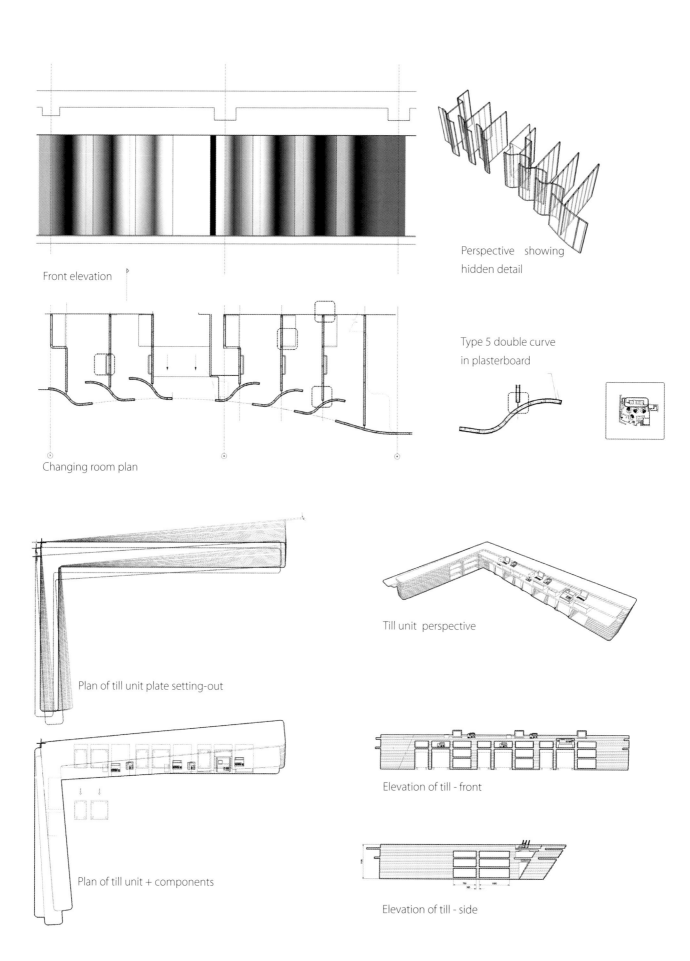

Front elevation

Perspective showing hidden detail

Changing room plan

Type 5 double curve in plasterboard

Plan of till unit plate setting-out

Till unit perspective

Plan of till unit + components

Elevation of till - front

Elevation of till - side

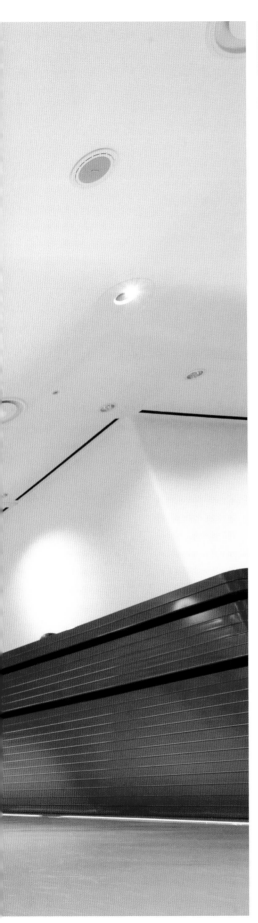

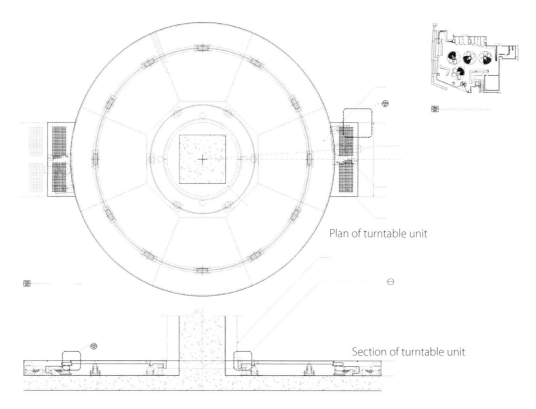

Plan of turntable unit

Section of turntable unit

273

Massimiliano & Doriana Fuksas

Emporio Armani Chater Road

Hong Kong

Photographs: Ramón Prat

Architecture:
Massimiliano & Doriana Fuksas

The new Armani Store / Chater Road development will be the biggest Armani retail location in the world after Milan's Armani / Via Manzoni, and is inteded to be a meeting point for people and a way of life, bringing together clothing, accessories, eyewear, watches, jewellery, cosmetics, fragrances, books, flowers and Italian cuisine under one roof. Located at Hong Kong Central at the junction between Chater Road, where the Giorgio Armani boutique has pavement frontage, and Pedder Street, onto which both Emporio Armani and the Emporio Armani Caffè face, linked by the pedestrian bridges leading to the Central Business District along which one million people transit each day.

The building is on three levels and has a surface area of 3,300 square metres of which 2,100 square meters (22,600 sqft) are retail space.

Soft, sophisticated and elegant the warm cream colour of St. Maximin stone is contrasted by furniture and fixtures in ebony and macassar wood, with hangers and fittings in burnished brass. The lighting design plays with shadow and light creating focused spaces and sensations. Invisible recessed lamps, transformed into spotlights, trace the contours or aim directly at the garments and objects on display, while versatile light fixtures appear to blend in with the surrounding space. A dramatic staircase, an architectural feature of Giorgio Armani boutiques leads one effortlessly between floors. Is composed of two sheets of stainless steel on which the panels of glass are mounted; the handrail is stainless steel covered by a tube in transparent plexiglass.

The leitmotif for the store is glass with a darting red ribbon, a sort of line, an automatic writing embracing and keeping together all the shop of light or the Emporio Armani store facing onto Pedar Street with its bustling streets and bridges. Fuksas's have literally freed the structure of the space from weight and mass by using treated, sometimes curved, glass throughout to project rippling reflections as if water is flowing from the walls. Each pillar becomes a source of light along with the walls which are embedded with fibre optic filaments. The resined glass floors and glass staircase add to the overall sense of lightness.

The project develops around the concept of fluidity, studying the paths of the visitors and their casual movements. These invisible paths construct the very base of the exhibition space.

GROUND LEVEL
Giorgio Armani Women's and Men's Collections (750 m2)

SECOND LEVEL
Emporio Armani Women's and Men's Collections (500 m2)
AJ|Armani Jeans Women's and Men's Collections (280 m2)
Emporio Armani Caffè (510 m2)
Armani Casa (270 m2)

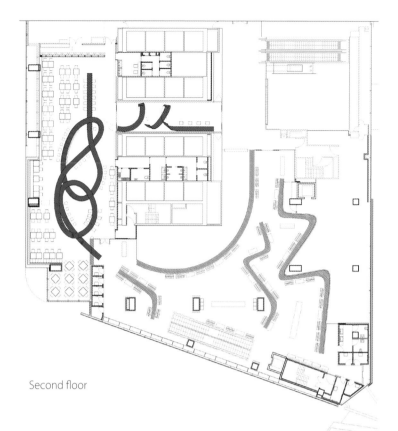

Second floor

The space in Armani Libri is defined by sliding panels which allow a view from the exterior, by display walls in satin plexiglass and stainless steel and the colors of the shelves alternate between red and white.

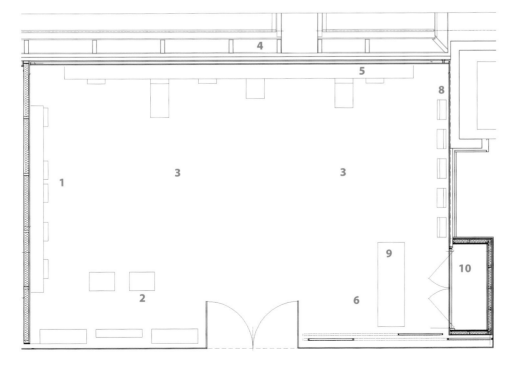

BOOK SHOP PLAN
1. Book shelf
2. Front book display
3. Book display table
4. Polycarbonate 5 mm
   MDF 12 mm
   RHS 80 x 30
   Pack-out from wall
   Surface 13 mm
5. Reading table
6. Sliding panel
7. Polycarbonate 5 mm
   MDF 12 mm
   Pack-out from wall
   Surface 20 mm
8. Magazine recks
9. Cashier desk
10. Stock room

The furniture, as shown in the cosmetics shop, is all designed by Massimiliano and Doriana Fuksas in satin stainless steel clad in soft and translucent plexiglass. The resined glass floors and glass display cases add to the overall sense of lightness.

Transparent plexiglass vases lend the shop area a sense of
extreme lightness and create the illusion that the flowers are
floating. (design by Monte di Rovello).

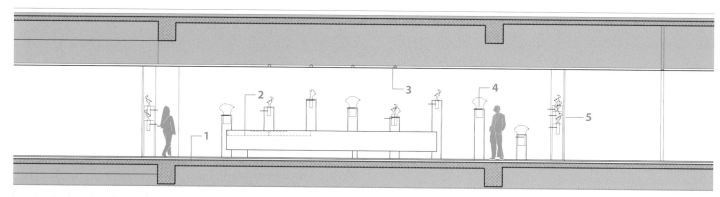

Longitudinal section flower shop

1. Epoxi Resin, 6 mm
   Self-leveling layer, 30 mm
   Mortar, 65 mm
2. Slate table
3. Recessed downlight
4. Polycarbonate display case
5. Glass case

Cross section flower shop

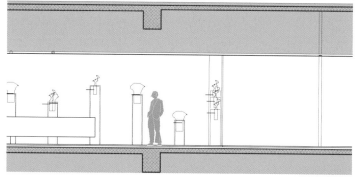

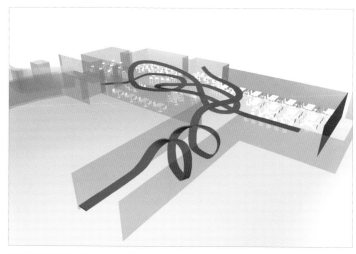

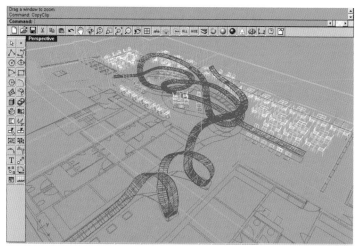

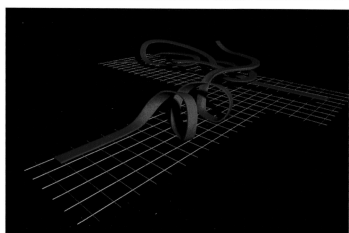

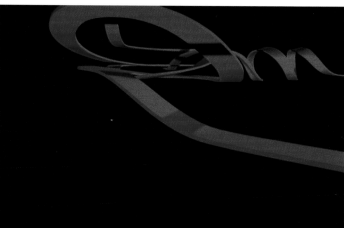

The cafeteria, with seating for 140 people, is unforgettable. Continuing the store's leitmotif a red strip of fiberglass twists and turns mimicking a roller-coaster ride creating tables, bars and a living sculpture as it runs its course through the space.

Gordon Kipping & Frank O. Gehry

Issey Miyake Tribeca

York City, USA

Photographs: Paul Warchol, Gordon Kipping

Located on 119 Hudson Street at the corner of N. Moore Street, this is a new showcase for Issey Miyake Men's and Women's collections. The shop was designed by architect Gordon Kipping, principal of the New York City office of G TECTS LLC. Miyake, always fascinated by Gehry's vision and approach, contacted the architect who agreed to sign on in conjunction with Kipping.

The design was born after Miyake's visit to the Gehry studio in Los Angeles, where he described his vision of a Gehry "tornado" whipping through the space and transforming everything in its path.

The original warehouse building was designed by the prominent New York architect Thomas R. Jackson and completed in 1888. G TECTS LLC led a team of preservation experts and conservation consultants to determine the building's original condition and direct the subsequent restoration, primarily of the façade. The use of glass is extensive throughout the project. Transparency enabled spatial and programmatic connections where vertical separation and security concerns necessitated physical separation. The removal of the original wood plank flooring to expose the original building joists enabled the insertion of a new glass box building into the cellar floor. To emphasize this new construction, a five foot wide border of glass flooring was inserted between the glass box and the existing structure.

The cash desk is a double-cantilevered stainless steel box hovering precariously over the glass floor border. Stainless steel display platforms on concealed wheels contain stock in drawers and alternately function as runways for the presentation of collections. Glass display cases and shelving offer display for more precious merchandise.

Alejandro Gehry produced two murals for the project. Inspired by his father's architecture and Miyake's clothing, and with elements of his own personal style thrown into the mix, the hand-drawn and computer manipulated collages serve to draw the eye to the farthest reaches of the retail area, down to the cellar lounge and back to the turbulent sprawl of his father's sculpture. The murals mark a gallery space that will feature a rotating display of work by young artists.

Photographs:
Paul Warchol, Gordon Kipping

Architecture:
Gordon Kipping & Frank O. Gehry

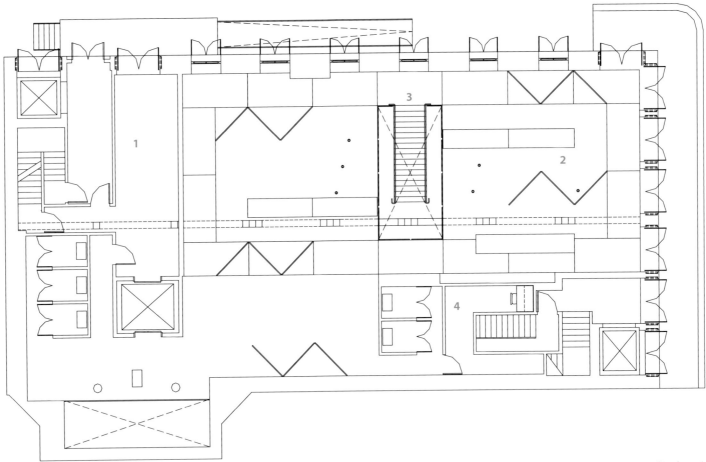

Ground floor plan

1. Entrance lobby
2. Showroom
3. Stairway
4. Offices
5. Collections
6. Reception
7. Customer lounge
8. Toilets
9. Press
10. Fitting room
11. Administration

The ground floor is the main selling area with 270 sqm (2,900 sqft) of retail space, with the rest of the space dedicated to storage and service space and the entrance lobby. The cellar floor features a 700 sqft showroom, ample retail space and a customer lounge.

Part of Frank Gehry's titanium 'tornado' sculpture is seen on the preceding page. The piece extends from a shaft emerging from the cellar floor to a turbulent sprawl engulfing the ceiling of the ground floor. Built from ultra-thin gauge titanium, it was shipped to the site in flat 4 x 8 foot sheets. There, Gordon Kipping and a team of architect volunteers bent it to match the project model and adhered it to a steel armature with Velcro pads.

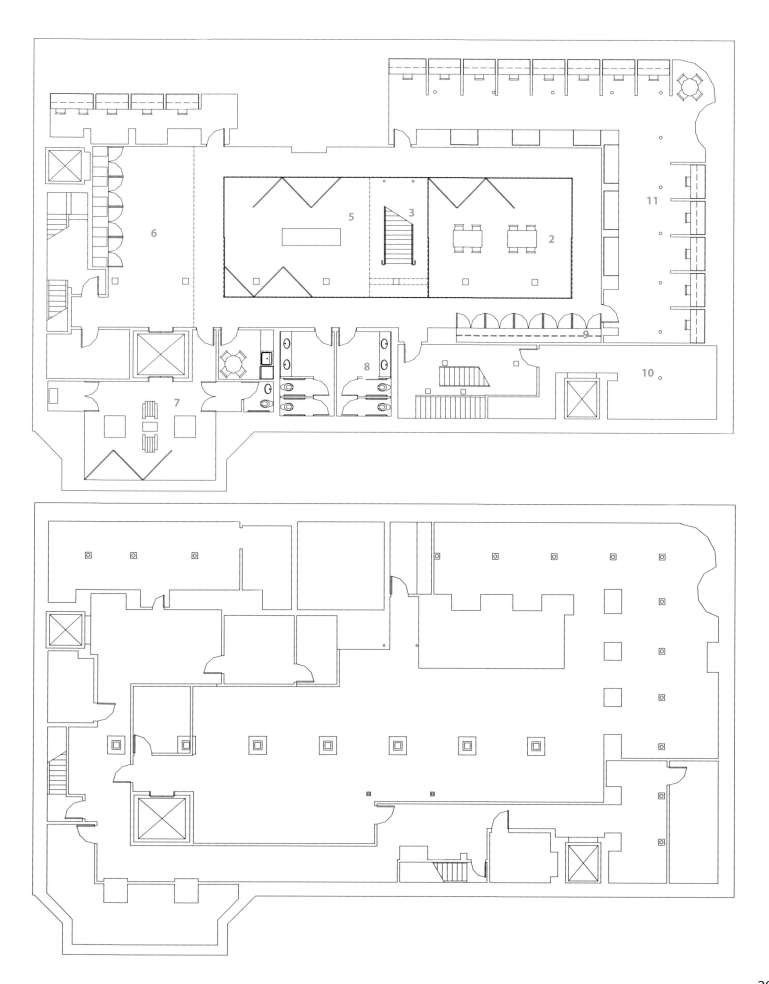

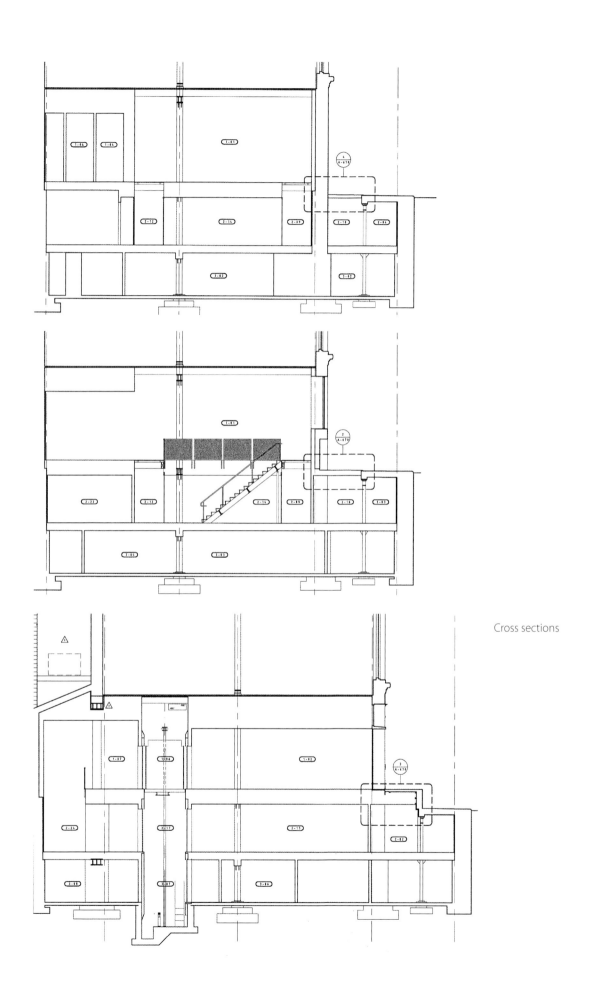

Cross sections

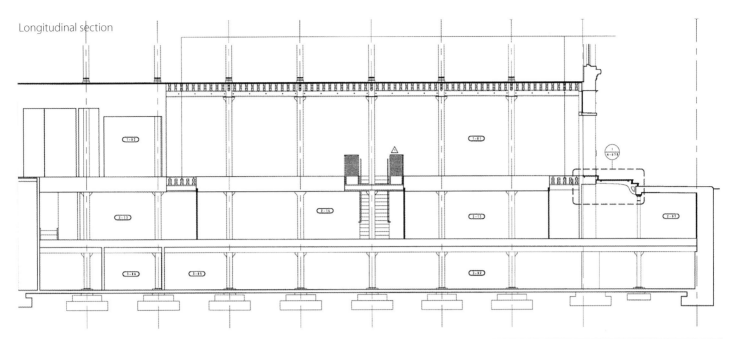

Support detail, section

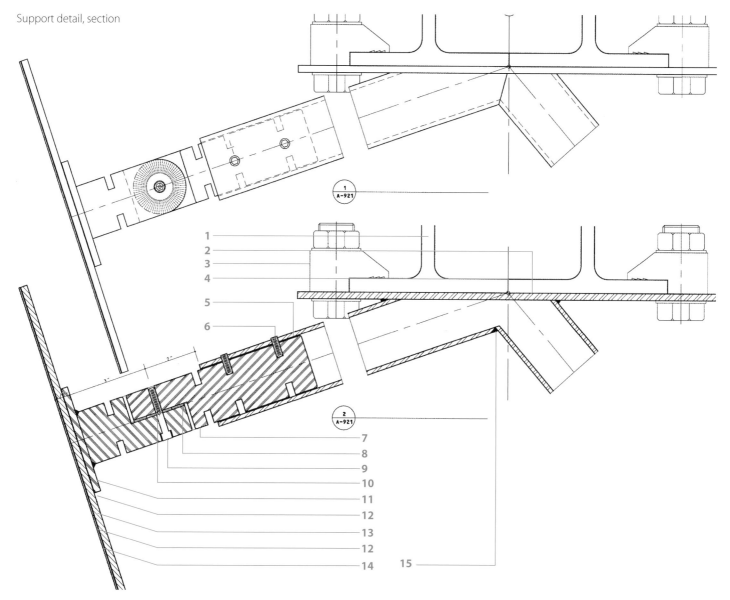

1. Existing cast iron beam

2. Steel plate

3. Type B MLB100 clamp by lindapter

4. Point of intersection of secondary support, centerline & cast iron beam

5. Secondary support, 2"dia. Schedule 40 steel pipe

6. ¼"-20 dia. by ¾" long socket set screw, w/ ratchet locking action

7. Stainless steel 2 piece elbow

8. Adjacent elbow surfaces w/ radial saw tooth serration

9. ¼"-20 dia. by 2" long socket head cap screw

10. Point of projected intersection of secondary support centerline & elbow pivot point

11. ¼" stainless steel plate

12. Adhesive

13. ¼" neoprene sheet

14. Industrial Velcro pad

15. Full penetration groove weld all around

16. Point of projected intersection of primary & secondary support centerlines

17. Primary support

Support detail, elevation and section

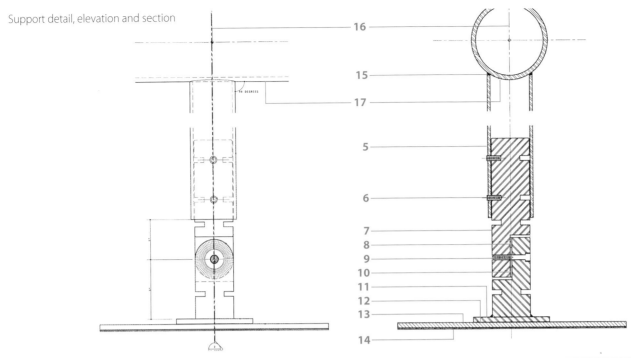

16
15
17
5
6
7
8
9
10
11
12
13
14